In Christ Alone

A Look at Blessings in Ephesians 1

Radiant Study Series

Edited by
Autumn Richardson
and
Melissa McFerrin

CYPRESS

Copyright © 2023 by Autumn Richardson

Manufactured in the United States of America

Cataloging-in-Publication Data

In Christ alone: a look at blessings in Ephesians 1. Radiant study series/ edited by Autumn Richardson and Melissa McFerrin.

p. cm.

Includes scripture index.

ISBN 978-1-956811-39-1 (pbk.) 978-1-956811-40-7 (ebook)

1. Bible. Ephesians I—Study and teaching. I. Richardson, Autumn, editor.

II. McFerrin, Melissa, editor. III. Title. IV. Series

227.5007—dc20

Library of Congress Control Number: 2023939530

For information:

Cypress Publications
3625 Helton Drive
PO Box HCU
Florence, AL 35630

www.hcu.edu

Contents

How To Use This Book

In Christ Alone is an in-depth study of the blessings found only in Christ, as listed in Ephesians 1. Before embarking on this study, I would encourage you to read the entire book of Ephesians. It will take you only around ten minutes. I would also encourage you to read the Introduction, as it will give you some background and context information that will help frame this study.

This book is suitable for group or individual study, with several tools provided to enhance the content of each chapter. There is a reading plan in the back of the book that will take you through the entire book of Ephesians in thirteen weeks. You can use it as a reading guide or as a Scripture copying schedule. The rest of the tools are available at the end of each chapter as well as in the appendices at the back of the book. You will find reflection questions that can be used in discussion settings or as journal prompts if studying on your own. There is also a prayer provided that is specific to the blessing of each chapter. Finally, there is a Bible marking plan for doing a topical study on the blessings from each chapter. Use the tools that work for your situation. I want this book to be versatile, helpful, and impactful for your walk with Christ as you grow more mature in Him.

Introduction

Autumn Richardson and Melissa McFerrin

"Bless" is a word I fear we have flippantly overused and watered down in modern Western culture. We use it in hashtags, on home decor, when someone sneezes, and to sign off on emails. Some even use it to politely brag about their lives. Blessings in Scripture are not so focused on what we have and what we do, but on God. Numbers 6:24–26 contains the well-known benediction that begins, "The Lord bless you and keep you. ..." What follows is a blessing that comes in the form of (1) God's presence and (2) what God does.[1] This book is meant to help us reclaim the biblical use of the word "blessed" and to help us acknowledge that the spiritual blessings from God through Christ far outweigh the temporal things we have in our lives.

Before embarking on our deep dive into the blessings found in Christ in Ephesians 1, it is wise to back up and look at the big picture of the letter in which these blessings are mentioned. While it would be improper to rank books of the New Testament, it would also be irresponsible to downplay the importance and impact of the book of Ephesians. The city of Ephesus was a major hub in what is now Turkey, and it was also vitally important in the infancy of the church. Many key players in the early church either lived or spent time in Ephesus. This letter from Paul is a model epistle in form and content and is still very relevant to the modern Christian. Looking at these elements and connecting the dots between Ephesians, Acts, and other New Testament books will enrich your study of this powerful little letter.

THE CITY

Asian peoples lived in the region of Ephesus as early as the second millennium B.C., but in 1044 B.C. Ionian Greeks established the city. Ephesus existed on its own before, from the sixth to fourth centuries B.C., it passed through the control of various powers. In 350 B.C. construction began on the impressive temple of Artemis.[2]

In 334 B.C. Alexander the Great conquered Ephesus and funded the remainder of the temple of Artemis. After Alexander's death, his general Lysimachus inherited Ephesus. He made renovations on the city from 286 to 281 B.C., which included enclosing it with a six-mile-long wall.[3] The Seleucids of Syria then took the city. In 189 B.C. Rome gained control and gave Ephesus to Eumenes

II, king of Pergamum. In 133 B.C. Attalus III Philometor, the last Pergamene king, returned the city to Rome.

During the early first century B.C., Ephesus, along with the rest of Asia Minor, suffered at the hands of the Romans. After Julius Caesar was assassinated in 44 B.C., Marc Antony taxed Ephesus at ten times the usual rate to fund his fight for control of Rome.[4] However, when Augustus became ruler of Rome in 31 B.C., Ephesus began to flourish. In 3 B.C. its triumphal arch was erected. At some point during the first century, Ephesus replaced Pergamum as capital of the Roman province of Asia. The Greek geographer Strabo called it "the largest emporium in Asia this side of the Taurus [Mountains]."[5] In A.D. 65 the governor of Asia restored the waterway to the harbor, facilitating trade. From the first to the fifth centuries the city hosted several ecumenical councils.

The exact location of Ephesus sometimes shifted as the city changed hands. Lysimachus moved the entire city from its original location to a nearby site between two hills.[6] By the first century, Ephesus was firmly established along the western edge of Asia Minor on the coast of the Aegean Sea. It was about three miles inland along the Cayster River and sported its own harbor. Because it was accessible to ships and strategically situated along the "common route" between Rome and Asia, Ephesus became an important center of commerce and culture. The city of Ephesus owned a vast amount of its surrounding land.

The great amphitheater in Ephesus, which could seat 25,000 people, was carved into the side of Mount Pion. Archaeologists have also discovered the triumphal arch, gymnasiums, theaters, the temple of Artemis, other temples, shrines, the civic agora, the commercial agora, shops, baths, public latrines, the city gates, burial monuments, catacombs, and a piped drainage system.[7] From Acts 18:19, it is clear that Ephesus also had a synagogue, and Acts 19:9 mentions the school of Tyrannus.

Ephesus boasted the fifth-largest population in the first-century world and the largest in Asia Minor, numbering approximately 400,000.[8] It enjoyed the status of a free city, meaning that, although it was officially under Roman rule, its own citizens governed it. The Ephesian government had a senate, an assembly, a Greek constitution, and the rare authority to carry out capital punishment. As members of a free city, citizens of Ephesus did not automatically become citizens of Rome.[9] Nonetheless, Ephesus was home to a number of Roman citizens, some of whom were part of the aristocracy and influential in local politics. As with its other free cities, Rome maintained a nominal presence in Ephesus to ensure that it acted in accordance with the interests of the empire.

Ephesus saw traffic from all parts of the inhabited world, and it also maintained an active slave market. These factors contributed towards the diversity of the city. Its inhabitants were of various ethnic and cultural backgrounds, including Greek, Roman, Asian, and Jewish.[10] Notably, Jews enjoyed certain religious privileges. In 14 B.C. Herod Agrippa sent a letter to Ephesus giving its Jews the right to collect money for the temple in Jerusalem and protecting them from being summoned to court on the Sabbath.[11] Roman citizens in Ephesus who were Jews were exempted from mandatory military service. Jewish beliefs and privileges occasionally created conflict between the Jewish and Gentile populations of Ephesus, as evidenced by ancient official documents addressing these concerns.

Ephesus embraced a variety of religious beliefs and practices, from emperor worship and magical arts to Judaism.[12] There was, of course, a significant following of the goddess Artemis. Evidence suggests that the Egyptian god Serapis also had a small cult there along with several other pagan deities.[13] Later, Christianity earned a place among the religions of Ephesus.

THE PEOPLE

The establishment of the church in Ephesus did not occur until around A.D. 52, near the end of the apostle Paul's second missionary journey.[14] Earlier, Paul, Silas, and Timothy had been "forbidden by the Holy Spirit to speak the word in Asia," so they passed along the edge of the province (Acts 16:6, NASB1995). After visiting several other cities, Paul collected Aquila and Priscilla and possibly Gaius, whom he had baptized in Corinth (1

Cor 1:14), and traveled to Ephesus (Acts 18:20–21). As far as can be determined from the biblical record, this team was the first to share the gospel with the Ephesians. The Jews there entreated Paul to continue to teach them, a rare request, but it appears that he stayed no longer than a few days. After he had made some converts, he left Ephesus in the hands of Aquila, Priscilla, and the new Christians, and he returned to Antioch.

The next mention of Christianity in Ephesus is found in Acts 18:24–26, which introduces Apollos. Apollos continued to work with the Ephesian congregation for some time; 1 Corinthians 16:12 seems to indicate that he was still there when Paul returned. It was probably through Apollos' early efforts that the twelve men were converted whom Paul met on his second visit.[15] At the least, Apollos converted a few believers who commended him to those in Achaia (Acts 18:27).

Aquila and Priscilla served an often-overlooked role in the growth of the church in Ephesus. Paul wrote that the church met in their house (1 Cor 16:19). When Paul was there, they supported him. When Apollos came, they encouraged him. Much is to be said for their knowledge of the Scriptures that they were able to teach such a learned man.[16] This couple would have provided the spiritual maturity and doctrinal soundness that the young church needed.

Around A.D. 53, during his third missionary journey, Paul returned to Ephesus, taking along Gaius and Aristarchus (Acts 19:1–7). He taught for three months in the synagogue, but when some unbelievers began to slander "the Way," he moved to the school of Tyrannus (Acts 19:8-9). Perhaps Tyrannus was a teacher or owner of the building who was sympathetic to their cause. After three months, Paul was drawing multitudes to hear the word (Acts 19:9), and after two years, even his enemies admitted that "in almost all of Asia, this Paul has persuaded ... a considerable number of people" (Acts 19:10, 26). He worked in Ephesus for about three years, the longest he stayed in any one city.

Much happened in those three years. Acts 19:13-16 tells of seven sons of a Jewish high priest who were battered by a man with an evil spirit when they attempted to cast it out. Inadvertently, they helped to spread Christianity, as "this became known to all, both Jews and Greeks, who lived in Ephesus; and fear fell upon them all and the name of the Lord Jesus was being magnified" (Acts 19:17). A number of pagan magicians converted, publicly burning their magic books, "so the word of the Lord was growing mightily and prevailing" (Acts 19:19-20).

The number of Gentiles turning to Christianity incited the most serious uprising yet against the Ephesian church. Demetrius and other craftsmen began a riot (Acts 19:24-41). Assistance came from an unlikely source in the form of the town clerk. This incident reveals the impact that Christianity was making on the town of Ephesus: it was enough to affect the economy of a huge city and to involve most of its people in an uproar. As a result, the church came under public scrutiny.

At Paul's urging, Timothy joined him in Ephesus. Timothy's primary contribution to the growth of the church, however, would come after Paul had left. Timothy's shared Jewish and Gentile heritage made him uniquely suited to work with the multicultural Ephesian congregation. The Ephesian Christians had seen how older Christians were supposed to behave, and Timothy showed them how a younger man should conduct himself. In addition to providing an example, he was responsible for continuing to preach the gospel (2 Tim 4:2), explaining the leadership roles of the congregation (1 Tim 3:1–13), refuting false doctrine (1 Tim 1:3), and teaching righteous living (1 Tim 4:12).

Paul wrote two letters to Timothy, instructing and encouraging him, and these letters reveal the state of the Ephesian congregation. The church in Ephesus was reaching the point of becoming self-governing and self-supporting.

After his three-year stay, Paul had contact with Christians at Ephesus once more in person (Acts 20:17–36). At the time of his visit with the Ephesian elders, Paul had with him others who had labored in Ephesus, including Gaius, Aristarchus, and Timothy. In his letters to Timothy, Paul mentioned other workers in Ephesus: Onesiphorus, who had assisted Paul in other cities as well, and Tychicus, whom Paul had sent to Ephesus after he left there (2 Tim 1:16–18; 4:12). Aquila and Priscilla were still serving the Ephesian congregation (2 Tim 4:19). Titus, Sosthenes, and the apostle John also worked in Ephesus.[17] Although many of these are not mentioned as often as Paul or Timothy, their influence cannot be overlooked.

THE BOOK

Ephesians fits into the category of New Testament books often referred to as the Prison Epistles, most likely written by Paul, either when he was in jail in Caesarea (Acts 24:27) or when he was in Roman custody for alledgedly bringing a Gentile into the temple (Acts 21:28-29; 28:16).[18] The book contains six chapters and shares significant similarities and content with the shorter epistle to the Colossians.[19]

Paul wrote letters to many of the churches he had visited and a few he had not, usually to address specific issues in those congregations. These letters typically followed a basic formula:

- Greeting
- Benediction
- Doctrinal Teaching
- Practical Application
- Final Charge

Ephesians is no exception. The doctrinal teaching can be found in the first three chapters, with the practical teaching in the last three. The portion of Chapter 1 that will be the focus of our study is the benediction. In the Greek, verses 3-14 and 15-23 are one sentence each, with verses 3-14 being the longest sentence in the Bible at 202 Greek words. Paul's opening is longer than the usual "praise be to God" that was a Jewish custom grafted into the early Christian tradition and used in the other epistles.[20] Paul used the benediction in Ephesians to praise God for what He has done through Christ and the work of the Holy Spirit. It is a beautiful synopsis of the gospel story that we cannot help but respond to in some way.

A prominent theme of the letter to the Ephesians can be found in the transition point of the book between the doctrinal and practical—to walk in a way worthy of what God has done (Eph 4:1). Key words or phrases that speak to that idea and would be appropriate to mark in your Bible are:

- In Him/through Him (23x)
- Love (15x)
- Grace (12x, more than in any other NT book)
- Walk (7x)
- Riches (5x, all in the first half)

Though the word "bless" occurs only four times in two verses, there are more than fifty blessings for the Christian that can be found in the book of Ephesians.

It is easy to fall into the tendency of the to-do list. *Do these things for God because He said so. Do the right thing because it is the right thing to do. Am I doing enough for God, for church, for my family?* Paul spends the first half of his letter reminding us of what God, Christ, and the Holy Spirit have already DONE. Our lives are meant simply to be lived in response to that. And how much more joy there is in the do's and don'ts when we think of it that way! May we all live our lives in light of the blessings in Christ as we grow into full maturity through Him (Eph 4:13–15).

Chapter 1
Every Spiritual Blessing in Christ
Ephesians 1:3
Debbie Dupuy

ONE MAIN THING

Ephesians 1:3 explains that we are blessed "with every spiritual blessing in the heavenly places" (NKJV). So, what does the word "blessing" mean? The Greek word for "blessing" is the word *eulogia*, which means "benefit" or "to speak well of."[1] To help us understand in a simple manner: God is speaking good things about us and pronouncing blessings over us for our benefit. Let that sink into your soul. These "spiritual blessings" that Paul referred to were not just nice ideas. They were realities to him that were attached to real benefits when he lived in those blessings. And, dear sister, they are also real for us; we just forget to claim them.

INTRODUCTION

I recently came across the following sermon illustration:

A little boy came to the Washington Monument and noticed a guard standing by it. [The little boy said,] "I want to buy it." "How much do you have?" asked the guard. "Thirty-five cents." "You need to understand three things," the guard explained. "First, thirty-five cents is not enough to purchase the monument; in fact, thirty-five million dollars is not enough. Second, the Washington Monument is not for sale. And third, if you are a U.S. citizen, you already own it." We need to understand three things:

All of the money in the world is not enough to purchase spiritual blessings.

Spiritual blessings are not for sale.

If we are in Jesus Christ, we already have every spiritual blessing in the heavenly places in Christ.[2]

R. A. Torrey stated it this way: "Separate from Christ, standing upon our own merits there is nothing for us: united with Christ by a living faith 'in Christ,' 'every spiritual blessing' is ours."[3]

We typically think of "blessings" in terms of material, or physical, do we not? Good health, a house, a car, children, grandchildren, a job, a well-performing 401k? What are spiritual blessings?

Spiritual blessings are so much more! Spiritual blessings are administered in the spiritual realm and express "the fullness of blessing in God's gift of eternal life in Jesus Christ."[4] Have you ever stopped to think of all the spiritual blessings we enjoy because of Christ? These are blessings freely given to us as His children, and, sadly, those who do not know Christ cannot possess them.

We understand physical blessings. We can see them and touch them. So many people around the world do not have the luxury of physical blessings. My family and I have traveled to many places where physical needs are desperate, yet the people we encounter who belong to Christ are the most joyful, dedicated Christians we know. They know something so many in the developed Western world cannot fathom; they understand what it means to be spiritually blessed in Christ Jesus.

So many of our brothers and sisters living in Haiti lack food, a proper home to live in, running water, and so many other physical blessings that most of us enjoy, yet when they message us, they ask for prayers to help them point others to Christ or for a new pair of shoes so they can keep walking and spreading the good news of Christ. I do believe they understand spiritual blessings! They possess more than physical blessings; in fact, they are millionaires in spiritual blessings!

GOING DEEPER

Do you realize you are a millionaire in spiritual blessings? Do you believe that every promise and benefit named for you is yours to enjoy? Paul explains that every marvelous spiritual blessing is assured to every believer in Christ Jesus, and these blessings flow from God's grace, wisdom, and eternal purposes. When we are united with Christ through baptism, every spiritual blessing is ours to enjoy at the time of our salvation.

I believe it is difficult for us, living in the physical realm, to understand the spiritual blessings we possess. These are not things we can purchase, see, or touch, but things our soul and spirit can know. Psalm 104:28 assures us that God opens His hand and satisfies His children with good things. The Bible is filled with promises that affirm an endless supply of riches, privileges, and blessings that we have never claimed. There are levels of peace, joy, security, hope, and answers to prayers awaiting us. We have inherited a fortune beyond anything we can imagine through the "spiritual blessings" in Christ.

I love the way F. F. Bruce describes this eulogy (blessing) in his commentary on the book of John. He explains that the followers of Christ draw from the ocean of divine fullness, grace upon grace—one wave of grace being constantly replaced by a fresh one. Think of the ocean surf—one wave of spiritual blessings coming after another in endless succession.[5] It is like the clouds of Noah's day that kept pouring out rain, the granaries in Joseph's days that held endless reserves of grain, the rock in the wilderness that kept pouring out water, the oil in Elijah's time that kept issuing oil, and the overflowing cup of blessings in Psalm 23.

Let us imagine something a little morbid for a moment. Think of your own funeral. Imagine there are several speakers at your funeral, proclaiming your faithfulness and love for others. Imagine that everything that is said about you is because you have every spiritual blessing in Christ. As each speaker stands to eulogize you, they mention each spiritual blessing from God to you.

The first speaker tells that you were *chosen* before the foundation of the world (Eph 1:4) and that your existence was not by accident or a by-product of natural selection. God had been thinking about your destiny before He ever said, "Let there be light" (Gen 1:3). Your life had a specific purpose on this earth because you were *chosen by Him.*

The second speaker stands and explains that you were *holy and blameless in Christ* (Eph 1:4), and that means you were fit to serve Him and worship Him in spite of your shortcomings. Because you were holy and blameless, when God saw you, He saw the loveliness of Christ in you. Your friend goes on to say that you were *in His love* (Eph 1:4). This love is *agape*, or unconditional love. You did not earn it. His love was bestowed on you as a spiritual blessing just because He created you, and you belong to Him.

Another friend comes forward to eulogize your life. This friend stands to speak of how you were *predestined to adoption* (Eph 1:5). Your friend explains that He accepted you to be His child and that you became part of His family. Many times during an adoption process, parents select the children they want to adopt, but God decided to adopt you before the foundation of the world! Wow— the audience is amazed! This friend goes on to explain that you were *accepted in the Beloved* (Eph 1:6). You were not rejected, nor an outcast, but instead you received His approval.

A fourth person stands and speaks of how you had *redemption through His blood* (Eph 1:7). Without His blood, you were a slave to sin and death, but through Christ, His blood was the price for your freedom from the chains of sin and death. You had the spiritual blessing of *forgiveness* (Eph 1:7). When you turned against God morally, or you consciously rebelled against His law, He still forgave you! The audience wipes tears of joy to think of your freedom through His redemption and forgiveness.

The fifth and final speaker stands at the podium and proclaims a wealth of your spiritual blessings. The audience is astounded. Dumbstruck! This friend tells of how His *grace* abounded in your life (Eph 1:7–8), and that means you had unmerited favor in abundance. When He revealed *the mystery of His will* (Eph 1:9), you came to understand that because of sin in this fallen world, where death, disease, and bad things happen to good people, there is a solution to our broken human condition. It is all wrapped up in Christ; He is the solution. This friend goes on to say that you received *an eternal inheritance* (Eph 1:11) and that "God will wipe away every tear from their eyes; there shall be no more death, nor sorrow, nor crying. There shall be no more pain, for the former things have passed away" (Rev 21:4).

Your friend continues with other spiritual blessings you received. This friend mentions *the word of truth* (Eph 1:13) that guided your life and helped you make important decisions. You were not left in the dark; in fact, you had an instruction manual for life. You were *sealed with the Holy Spirit* as a guarantee of your salvation (Eph 1:13). When there is a guarantee, that is assurance! You also received *the hope of His calling* (Eph 1:18), meaning that His calling for your life was the basket you could put all your eggs in. You had an Anchor and a Rock. Having the *riches of His inheritance* (Eph 1:18) means that you were valuable in Christ; you had the righteousness of God in Christ. You were His eternal possession whom He cherishes, and that is only the beginning! There is more!

You possessed *the exceeding greatness of His power* (Eph 1:19)! Paul says that "the exceeding greatness of His power [is] toward us who believe" (Eph 1:19). What kind of power of this? It is the same power that raised Christ from the dead! It is the same power that conquered sin, death, and hell. In Christ, this same power is present in your life today!

WRAPPING IT UP

As the funeral concludes, some are reminded of how spiritually blessed they are! Others, who do not know Christ, are asking the Christians in attendance to show them how they can become a spiritual millionaire like you!

The beautiful message for us is that we do not have to wait until we die to receive spiritual blessings. We do not need thirty-five million dollars, because they are not for sale! If we are in Christ, we can claim them now!

So, I have just one question for you: *Are you blessed today?*

PRAYER

God, thank You for blessing me. I know I have done nothing to deserve Your bountiful gifts. Help me to place more value on the spiritual blessings I have received than the physical things I can see with my eyes. Thank you for Jesus, who made it possible for me to partake in such wonderful, eternal blessings.

QUESTIONS

1. How does thinking of the definition of the Greek word *eulogia* challenge the Western concept of being blessed?
2. If you are in Christ, the blessings of Ephesians 1 are already yours. Which blessings do you need to more fully recognize and thank God for?
3. We often have a tendency to refer to blessings as the physical things in life. Why can this be problematic? What intentional actions can you

take to be more aware of your spiritual blessings?

4. If all your physical blessings were taken away tomorrow, would you be content with your spiritual blessings alone?

Chapter 2

Adoption

Ephesians 1:4-5

Jodi Gallagher

ONE MAIN THING

We should know God, so we can respond to others as He would. Nothing we do can take away our sonship in Christ if we ask for forgiveness.

INTRODUCTION

There's nothing sweeter than hearing the words, "Mama, can I hug you?" Coming from a newly adopted daughter who's been in your home for about a year and with whom you've struggled to build a relationship, these words may bring tears to your eyes. Perhaps a warm embrace will help build the loving connection that you want with your child. Or, it just may be that you gently squeeze your daughter's stiffened arms and body, while she is standing like a statue, giving no hug in return. Those are the moments when you'll realize that connecting with children through adoption is often much harder than Hollywood depicts.

That's adoption, at least, in my experience. There is no automatic bond that is created when papers are signed. To follow the example of our Lord, we must love even when it hurts.

GOING DEEPER

It was a call I will never forget. The man on the other end of the phone was telling me, "We had hoped you would adopt them." My husband and I were in the midst of our first foster care placement. We had decided to foster children with a view toward adoption. So, we had taken in three brothers (ages five, four, and nine months), meaning that in our moderately-sized, three-bedroom house, our three biological children (ages eleven, eight, and six) all had to cram into one room. That was the most intense six weeks of our lives. We had gotten in way over our heads, and we finally decided to give up those boys. The man on the phone was the boys' grandfather, encouraging us to change our minds. It was all far more than I could handle at the time, a very difficult decision. It became even more heart wrenching when, at the Department of Human Resources office, the four-year-old clung to me, begging me not to leave. I hate thinking back to that day.

So, what did I learn from that experience? Commitment. My husband and I vowed never to do that again, never to put other children in that situation. Whoever came into our house (only one at a time from now on!) would not leave due to our choice. It was a difficult time, but it has proven to be a valuable experience to have had, for the sake of future children placed into our home.

"He predestined us to adoption as sons..." (Eph 1:5 NASB1995).

We now have three adopted children in our home, biological siblings, who came into our house one at a time—first a boy, then his older sister, and then their newborn sister. My son's story began with several different placements in foster care. He had been passed from foster home to foster home. When he arrived at our house at age four, I could tell he had some struggles. He moved differently, and he had learning difficulties. One day I sat with my newly adopted son in a waiting room at the doctors' office. We had made the two-hour trip for doctors' appointments, surgeries, and lab work many times for over a year, trying to figure out what was the cause of my son's health concerns—but this day was different. Today we were seeing a geneticist, who, after spending only a few minutes observing him, diagnosed him with the terminal disease Duchenne Muscular Dystrophy (DMD). Jerry Lewis and his MDA telethons immediately popped into my mind. Though I knew nothing about DMD, I quickly learned what my son's future health would probably look like.

"He predestined us to adoption as sons..." (Eph 1:5).

A little over a year later, we adopted my son's six-year-old biological sister. Hers is a story of extreme trauma

—trauma hidden from us, perhaps locked only in her memory. It has been a struggle to connect with her, and she has been unable to meet the benchmarks of growth and maturity for children her age. When attempting to communicate with her, we are met with stares. She has been a part of the family for nearly five years now, yet some days seem as if we're starting from scratch.

"He predestined us to adoption as sons…" (Eph 1:5).

So, what can we learn from earthly adoption that can help us appreciate the spiritual adoption we receive from God? There are several things.

Commitment

We first can clearly see that our earthly experience with adoption can help us to understand the commitment we spiritually receive from God. Earthly adoption requires a commitment to keeping the children you are placed with no matter what baggage they have. Don't we all have baggage? God responds to us with commitment. No matter what we bring to the relationship, He has promised that, if we are willing, He will be our spiritual Father. There are so many Scriptures that point us to this. Ephesians 1:5 assures us that God knew before we were even created that He would adopt us as His own if we chose to obey Him. Other passages give us similar assurances:

"We have obtained an inheritance, having been predestined according to His purpose who works all things after the counsel of His will" (Eph 1:11).

"That is, it is not the children of the flesh who are children of God, but the children of the promise are regarded as descendants" (Rom 9:8).

It's a beautiful thing to know that no matter what we do, God will hold to His promise, when we are ready to return to Him.

Love

Human adoption can also help us to appreciate God's unconditional love for us. Unconditional love has been something I've struggled to understand. I grew up in a church where it seems I was taught that God loves you when you are good. Moreover, I am a very emotionally-driven person; it's hard for me to understand love apart from a warm emotion—which I do not always feel. That can even carry over to my view of people. But unconditional love means just that: unconditional. When God tells us He loves us, He just does—no strings attached.

What does that look like in everyday life? I believe that part of the reason God sent my adopted children to me was to teach me unconditional love. My three oldest children, to whom I gave birth, are part of me physically. I carried them for nine months. I loved them immediately and easily. My adopted children require me to actively make choices that show my love to them. I have never enjoyed fixing hair, but now I must sit down for nearly an hour and wash, comb, and style my daughter's hair. I have a million things that need to be accomplished around the house, but I must stop and take time to massage my son's legs because they are in pain from his disease. Because I want them to have some form of success, right now I homeschool them so that I can give them one-on-one attention. These acts can easily be seen as a burden, but I must choose to see them as showing acts of God to my children. God is using me to do just that.

"See how great a love the Father has bestowed on us, that we would be called children of God; and such we are" (1 John 3:1).

The unconditional love that I must seek to show to all my children will inevitably enhance connection—not only my connection to my children, but also my connection to God my Father. It will not happen quickly, though. Connection may be the most difficult aspect of adoption, because I so often feel like I'm putting out demonstrations of love without receiving anything in return. I must be longsuffering like my Father is longsuffering. Connection, though extremely important, is a struggle. Oftentimes my efforts with my children seem to be in vain. Can God relate to that feeling with me? I know I can relate in my experience with God— sometimes I feel like connection with Him is so hard.

I cannot possibly know all of my adopted children's past experiences like God knows each of us, but I can still seek connection. Just like my experiences with my adopted children have been a daily attempt at connection, our connection with God must be practiced daily. I fail at my attempts with my children, just like I fail at my attempts with God. If I continue to practice acts of love, though, I will begin to look like my Brother and Father.

"For those whom He foreknew, He also predestined to become conformed to the image of His Son, so that He would be the firstborn among many brethren" (Rom 8:29).

Giving up Control

Adoption can also teach us to let go and let God take control of the relationship. When my adopted children came into my life, I felt as though my job was to fix their brokenness. If only I could find the perfect remedy to "cure" my son's disease, or maybe if I discovered the ideal exercises to mend my daughter's mental struggles, then we would be making some progress. However, after five-plus years of searching for the best solutions to all of my children's problems, I am slowly yielding to the notion that I can't fix my children, and I don't need to. I simply must love them and point them to Jesus daily through my love for them, because that's exactly what God does. He takes all of our brokenness and suffering and through His love leads us to lives beyond anything we could have imagined.

WRAPPING IT UP

Once we had adopted two children, because of the struggles we were facing with our new son and daughter, Ed and I decided to close our home to foster care and adoption and no longer take in any more children. God had other plans. In August of 2019, less than a year after our daughter's adoption, the Department of Human Resources called to tell us that our son and daughter's biological mother had given birth to a little girl and asked if we would take her—a new baby in the house! Ed and I were now forty and struggled to imagine starting over in raising a child. Besides that, we would need to start all over getting certified to be foster parents. After initially declining the offer, we welcomed her into our home at five weeks old and adopted her nearly two years later. She has been pure joy!

"He predestined us to adoption as sons ... according to the kind intention of His will" (Eph 1:5).

> Blessed be the God and Father of our Lord Jesus Christ, who according to His great mercy has caused us to be born again to a living hope through the resurrection of Jesus Christ from the dead, to obtain an inheritance which is imperishable and undefiled and will not fade away, reserved in heaven for you (1 Pet 1:3–4).

When I was a mother to only three children, I homeschooled them with the determination to give my kids the best education possible. Oh yes, learning the Bible was an important part of that, but looking back, I realize I wasn't able to make it a priority to live it out. The ambitions we instilled in our kids for academic and worldly success did not really reflect Scripture. God stepped in and gave me two sweet children who will most likely never graduate from high school, let alone attend college. My daughter will embrace me now—there's hope. My son must be shown how to live his life for God with this debilitating disease—there's hope. God has opened my eyes to seeing more clearly what matters most. I frequently fail, but I must do my best to be His image-bearer to all my children. I have hopes for all my children, and somehow it is less about the successes they'll have in life and more about how they'll all look like their Father. And we have the assurance that transformation is coming (Phil 3:21). There's hope!

PRAYER

Abba Father, thank You for making the decision to call me Your own. Thank You for showing me care and compassion as your child every day. Help me never to forget that I am Yours.

QUESTIONS

1. What baggage do you bring to your relationship with God?
2. How does it make you feel knowing that God is committed to us like a parent, no matter how broken or distant we might be?
3. Our adoption in Christ offers us continual connection to our Father. How does He continually reach out to us? What is our avenue for responding?
4. In what ways do you see God's deliberate love for you, His adopted child? How do your actions reflect gratitude for that love?

Chapter 3

Sanctification

Ephesians 1:4

Kim Chalmers

ONE MAIN THING

Sanctification. It is a word with a heavy meaning and great responsibility for the Christian. The word "sanctification" can be used as a noun or a verb. According to Merriam-Webster, as a noun, "sanctification" is "the state of growing in divine grace as a result of Christian commitment after baptism or conversion."[1] The verb "sanctify" is "to set apart to a sacred purpose," "to free from sin: purify."[2] First Thessalonians 4:7 states, "For God did not call us to be impure, but to live a holy life" (NIV). God wants us to live a godly life without impurity.

In Ephesians 1:4, Paul wrote to the church in Ephesus, "even as he chose us in him before the foundation of the world, that we should be holy and blameless before him" (ESV). As Christians, we are to be sanctified, holy, and blameless before Christ. Christ wants us at our absolute best. Sanctification begins at the point of baptism (1 Cor 6:11). As we live the Christian life, we are to be faithful unto death (Rev 2:10) and to strive to be sanctified. Satan is doing his best every day to influence us to be of the world. Jesus warns against this. In John 17:16-17, when praying to the Father, He said, "They are not of the world, just as I am not of the world. Sanctify them in the truth; your word is truth." He clearly states the only way we can be sanctified is through the truth which is God's word.

Sanctification is a lifelong process that Christians must work diligently to achieve on a daily basis. We are to become more Christlike every day, to leave the world—to be set apart. Philippians 1:6 reads, "And I am sure of this, that he who began a good work in you will bring to completion at the day of Jesus Christ." He is always working in our lives—if we let Him.

GOING DEEPER

For our discussion, I would like to focus on being sanctified in mind and heart. Our thoughts can keep us from being sanctified. Our hearts can keep us from being sanctified. Let us look more closely at practical ways we can keep our minds and hearts sanctified, so we may live the kind of life that God wants us to!

The Bible has much to say about having a pure mind and heart. A quick Internet search will give you about 200 verses on the importance of having a pure mind and heart. As a good Bible student knows, if the Holy Spirit included this much information about a subject, it is important.

According to the Cleveland Clinic, our brains process about 70,000 thoughts per day.[3] Now, this begs the question, what kind of thoughts are we having? When worldly or sinful thoughts enter our minds, this keeps us separated from Christ. The world we live in now has our minds bombarded with outside influences such as social media and just "noise" in general. The impact from COVID-19 on our mental state is now coming to the surface. The amount of information that our mind processes on a daily basis can be overwhelming. This can lead to thoughts which could take our focus off of Christ.

The Bible specifically discusses keeping the mind pure. Notable examples are Philippians 4:7, Romans 12:2, 1 Corinthians 2:16, Philippians 2:5, 1 Peter 1:13, and 2 Corinthians 10:3-5. In just a sampling of these verses, we see the same theme—to keep your mind on Christ. A widely-known verse dealing with the mind is Philippians 4:8:

> Finally, brothers and sisters, whatever is true, whatever is noble, whatever is right, whatever is pure, whatever is lovely, whatever is admirable—if anything is excellent or praiseworthy—think about such things (NIV).

This verse is filled with rich truths. The phrase "think about" in Greek means to take into account.[4] Paul is telling the church in Philippi that things that are true, noble, right, pure, lovely, admirable, excellent, praiseworthy—these are things that should fill our minds. If these concepts fill our minds daily, we are sanctified. Burton Coffman concludes,

> Thought control is clearly the practice Paul enjoined here. If people would live correctly in God's sight, let them think of those qualities which possess positive value. Thinking of such things will lead to speaking of them, as exemplified in the lives of associates, thus contributing to the joy and unity of Christian fellowship.[5]

Sanctification of the mind is growing in wisdom and knowledge in Christ. Colossians 3:10, Philippians 1:9, and Romans 12:2 all illustrate this point. We are to be renewed in knowledge and in our minds. We are to discern what is truth and what is not. God is all-knowing. He knows us—even the numbers of hairs on our heads (Matt 10:30), and He knows our thoughts (Isa 55:9). Whatever our thoughts are, He knows.

Laura Jenkins, in her book *Thought Garden*, equates our minds and thoughts to a garden. If you are a gardener, you know weeds are part of the gardening process. As God is the Master Gardener (John 15:1), He desires for us to take care of our thought gardens.[6] Jenkins sums up this concept perfectly:

Seeds are the thoughts in our thought gardens, and they are constantly being planted. They grow based on how we think, and what we think on most will grow. Some seeds produce healthy thoughts (think flowers) and others produce unhealthy thoughts (think weeds).[7]

She concludes that when we think negative thoughts (weeds) continually, these negative thoughts will take over our minds.

David Lipscomb concurs: "We cannot entertain impure thoughts without becoming corrupt, and we cannot think good thoughts without becoming pure."[8] When we think negative, worldly, sinful thoughts, these thoughts are what we will be consumed with. You cannot think two things (pure thoughts vs. worldly thoughts) at the same time, just as you cannot serve two masters (Matt 6:24). Everything good comes from God—even our thoughts (Jas 1:17).

Equally important as sanctification of the mind is sanctification of the heart. The Bible has much to say about purifying the heart. In Matthew 5:8, Christ tells us that "blessed are the pure in heart, for they shall see God." You cannot be in the presence of God without a pure heart. The psalmist wrote in Psalm 119:11, "I have stored up your word in my heart, that I might not sin against you" (ESV). Many attribute the authorship of this psalm to David. David knew the law, but from Scripture we know that he did not always submit. In order to sanctify our hearts, we must always be diligent in following God's word.

First Peter 3:15 reads,

> But in your hearts honor Christ the Lord as holy, always being prepared to make a defense to anyone who asks you for a reason for the hope that is in you; yet do it with gentleness and respect.

Our primary mode of communication with others is verbal. Our words can sometimes get us into trouble. The tongue can be a powerful force. Angry words can lead to confrontation with others in an ungodly and unsanctified way (1 Pet 3:10; Prov 15:28).

Let's look at Luke 6:43–46:

> For no good tree bears bad fruit, nor again does a bad tree bear good fruit, for each tree is known by its own fruit. For figs are not gathered from thornbushes, nor are grapes picked from a bramble bush. The good person out of the good treasure of his heart produces good, and the evil person out of his evil treasure produces evil, for out of the abundance of the heart his mouth speaks.

Paul David Tripp, in his book *War of Words: Getting to the Heart of Your Communication Struggles*, connects the fruit mentioned in this Scripture to our words. He concludes, "Jesus' brilliant metaphor reveals that our words are shaped and controlled by the thoughts and motives of our hearts."[9] What we have in our hearts will come out through our words. That is why it is so important to keep God's word in our hearts, so we may be sanctified in a sinful world. Jesus said it this way (a couple of times!): "For the mouth speaks what the heart is full of" (Matt 12:34; Luke 6:45 NIV). Dietrich Bonhoeffer offers sage advice:

> Often, we combat our evil thoughts most effectively if we absolutely refuse to allow them to be expressed in words. ... It must be a decisive rule of every Christian fellowship that each individual is prohibited from saying much that occurs to him.[10]

We all are subject to influences. Influences from our families, work, entertainment choices, and the world can be either good influences or bad ones. These influences can lead us to be sanctified or not. We see many examples from the Bible of those who influenced others. You can probably think of some of the bad influences. One that comes to mind is the story of King Rehoboam and the counsel he took from his friends. Because King Rehoboam chose to follow unwise counsel, he treated the ten northern tribes harshly, they rebelled against him, and he lost a portion of his kingdom (1 Kgs 12:1–17). When we allow others to influence our choices, we must make sure that counsel does not go against God.

Let us focus on an example of a good influence and how two women helped to sanctify the heart of individual. Timothy's grandmother Lois and mother Eunice come to mind as good influences. We read in 2 Timothy 1:5 of how these women were a great influence on young Timothy's faith. They instilled in him the love of Scripture, God, and doing the right thing. As a result, Timothy grew up to be an important influence by spreading the gospel to others. Life is much easier when we have wise, godly influences to rely on. God never meant for the Christian life to be lived alone without the encouragement of our brethren. Therefore, when we are the type of influence that God wants us to be, we can encourage others to live a sanctified life!

WRAPPING IT UP

We are sanctified when we say "yes" to God and "no" to sin. It is a process in our hearts and minds to desire to be Christlike. How often do we think about sanctification? Is it part of our daily awareness? How can we sanctify our minds and hearts? Here are just a few ways. Reflect on other ways and incorporate them into your life.

1. Have a solid prayer life. When we spend time in prayer, we can align our hearts and minds to the will of God. Notice the word "align." The purpose of praying is not to "get" what we want. The purpose is to offer adoration, confession, thanksgiving, and supplication and to submit

ourselves to the will of God. Jesus gave us a pattern of how to pray in Matthew 6:5–15. Through prayer, we will gain clarity about His will and how we can best serve Him.

2. Spend time in study of God's Word. Second Timothy 2:15 tells us to "Do your best to present yourself to God as one approved, a worker who has no need to be ashamed, rightly handling the word of truth" (ESV). Find time every day to read the Bible. We are blessed today that we have available to us excellent podcasts and Bible studies which are easy to access day or night. The more time you spend in God's word, the better equipped you are to sanctify your mind and heart.

3. Spend time in fellowship with other Christians. I have always said that you can't get to know people at church. Some may think that is an odd statement, but I believe really to fellowship and know other Christians, you need time outside of the church building to do that. Take the time to listen to and learn from other Christians. This involves getting to know them, their families, their hopes, and their dreams. Be a good Christian friend to someone.

4. Express gratitude. Show gratitude to Christ and to others. First Samuel 12:24 and 1 Thessalonians 5:18 are just a few examples of showing gratitude to God. We are nothing without His love and forgiveness. Express

gratitude to others so that your light may shine, and He may be glorified (Matt 5:15-16).

Sanctification, for us as Christians, is what keeps us separated from the world and close to God. The Bible enlightens us on ways we are to be sanctified in order to be Christlike. The study of sanctification can offer many avenues to consider. I believe that to be truly sanctified, it starts in the mind and heart. I pray that you will continue to study sanctification and become aware of the important role being set apart plays in our Christian life!

PRAYER

Holy God, sanctify me. Help my heart and my mind to think on You always. You have lifted me out of darkness, and I long to walk in Your holiness for the rest of my days. Cleanse me from all of my impurities.

QUESTIONS

1. Describe how sanctification is both a state of being for the Christian and also a never-ending process. In other words, how are you both *sanctified* and *being sanctified*?
2. What is keeping your heart and mind from being fully pure? What are you clinging to that is hindering your thoughts from remaining on Him and on righteousness?

3. Thinking about your sanctification through prayer, the word, fellowship, and gratefulness— which of these comes most naturally to you? Which do you need to be more intentional about making a part of your spiritual life?

4. What are some practical ways you choose to be "set apart" from the world? Are there certain activities you choose not to engage in? Places you won't go? What does the tension of "in the world but not of the world" look like in your life?

Chapter 4
Grace and Favor
Ephesians 1:5-8
Lori Tays

ONE MAIN THING

The book of Ephesians is flush with references to the great, abundant, overflowing richness of God's grace. The concept of grace is commonly described as "unmerited favor," and though this is not an inaccurate description, it surely seems sparse to encapsulate such a grand idea. What does grace actually *mean*? What does grace actually *do*? The first chapter of Ephesians provides the perfect starting place for understanding grace—the intersection where you and God meet.

GOING DEEPER

Ephesians 1 includes three specific references to grace. First, Paul's greeting to the Ephesians includes a blessing of "Grace and peace to you from God our Father and the Lord Jesus Christ" (Eph 1:2 NIV). He indicates that our calling and adoption are "to the praise of His glorious grace, which He has freely given us in the One He loves" (Eph 1:6). He continues by describing our redemptive message in a beautiful phrase: "In him we have redemption through his blood, the forgiveness of sins, in accordance with the riches of God's grace that he lavished on us" (Eph 1:7–8). Though several Greek words can be translated as the word "grace," the word used in each of these instances is *xáris*. HELPS Word Studies describes *xáris* as "favor, disposed to, inclined, favorable towards, leaning towards."[1]

This beautiful word picture indicates that your Creator is tender toward you. He is, by His nature, favorable toward you. He *leans toward* you, and this message is both refreshing and biblical. "I love the Lord because He hears my voice and my prayer for mercy," declares Psalm 116:1–2, "Because He bends down to listen, I will pray as long as I have breath!" (NLT). At its core, grace declares that God's natural position is one of rapt attentiveness. He kneels down to listen to what His children have to say. It invokes a sense of grandfatherly tenderness, of a Creator who desires to know you and actively works to be part of your life.

Perhaps unintentionally, many of us grew up with the sense of God as a sort of employer, with Christians as interviewees for the "job" of making it through the gates of heaven. He peers at us over the rim of His glasses, checklist in hand, waiting for us to make a mistake. Yet this is the farthest cry from the description found within these Scriptures. Instead, Paul paints a portrait of an extravagantly giving God leaning down, whispering words of encouragement, and cheering us along our journey. He is not an impassive observer, but an active participant in our lives.

Note the descriptive words connected to this word *xáris* in the Ephesians passages above. Here we see that grace is "freely given" (Eph 1:6). It is described as "riches" "lavished" upon us (Eph 1:7). These are words connected to the most luxurious of circumstances. Do you remember the little boy in the book *Charlie and the Chocolate Factory*? Poor, struggling, and mistreated, Charlie would have felt satisfied to win a single chocolate bar. He would have been over the moon to win a chocolate bar every day for the rest of his life. But Charlie received much more: Instead, he received the entire chocolate factory! This gift was lavish and extraordinary. This gift couldn't be held in his hands. Instead, the gift he was given was so great that he could live in it. He could move right in and make it his home.

In the same way, grace is not a gift so small that we can hold it in our hands. God's favor, His inclination toward us, is a place where we live. We are invited to move right in and make our home there. What a beautiful picture of His indescribable love for us! In addition, the concept of living inside this free and lavish grace is a simple way for us to understand what some call "the limits of grace." Is there a limit to the sin that grace will cover? Should I worry about whether grace is covering me at any given time on any given day? Or, in Paul's words, "Shall we go on sinning so that grace may increase?" (Rom 6:1 NIV).

The difference is this: You can drop a gift, and you may even break it, but you can't accidentally drop your house. You may lose a gift, but no one accidentally misplaces his or her home. You can *choose* to move out of a house. You can pack up your things and walk away, but you do it on purpose. In the same way, you can walk away from your God. You may decide that His teachings are too difficult. You may determine that something else is more important to you. You can walk away from His grace—but you do it on purpose. If you struggle with accepting the role that God's grace plays in your own life, take some time to consider where you're living. If you've moved out, checked out, burned out, then absolutely, choose to move back in. But if you're living in the grace you've been gifted, yet ever worrying that you're not enough— rest easy, friend. Our Father is leaning into *you*.

From the Garden of Eden, this beautiful picture of grace has threaded its way through every moment of human history. In His walking in the garden with Adam and Eve in the cool of the day, we see that our Father leaned towards them, finding pleasure in simply being with them. When Noah found grace and favor, God went to extraordinary lengths to save Noah and his family. He again showed His favor and lovingkindness to the Israelites in the wilderness through a fire burning brightly, guiding their path toward a lovingly-chosen homeland of their own. Christ's descent to live among us, as one of us, is the greatest symbol of leaning toward us. John 1:14 says, "And the Word became flesh and dwelt among us, and we have seen his glory, glory as of the only Son from the Father, full of grace and truth" (ESV). And though we don't know when this will be, He is already planning for a day when He will bring us home, closing that circle and bringing us back to full connectedness to Him. Peter notes this future grace in 1 Peter 1:13: "Therefore, prepare your minds for action, keep sober in spirit, fix your hope completely on the grace to be brought to you at the revelation of Jesus Christ" (NASB1995).

Consider this: The Creator God does indeed have a perfect place, a holy place, an eternal place where He lives. It's true that He could not bear to see us struggling down here alone. So, the Eternal wrapped Himself in our weak and mortal skin. He stripped Himself of every title and every jewel and every single comfort. He lived like us, and He hurt like us, and He suffered like us. And He did it all because He is so inclined toward us.

The richness of His grace toward us is truly beyond our ability to comprehend. It's expansive and wild and bigger than anything of our own imagining. Vance Havner says, "The grace of God transcends all our feeble efforts to describe it. It cannot be poured into any of our mental receptacles without running over."[2] Still, we see and understand that, against all reason, His grace has become ours. "Let us then approach God's throne of *grace* with confidence, so that we may receive mercy and find *grace* to help us in our time of need" (Heb 4:16 NIV, emphasis added).

WRAPPING IT UP

As we begin to scratch the surface of God's grace toward us, this understanding has the power to transform our interactions and relationships with others. In recognizing this concept of grace as a "leaning in," as a "leaning toward," we can also begin to understand that the embracing of grace is an embracing of God's ways and His word and His truth.

The power of fully-realized grace actually works inside us to change us into the people God desires us to be. Titus 2:11-12 says,

> For the grace of God has appeared that offers salvation to all people. It teaches us to say "No" to ungodliness and worldly passions, and to live self-controlled, upright and godly lives in this present age.

It is an ever-present teacher, guiding us into wise decisions and selfless living.

Understanding grace also gives us the ability to withstand whatever comes our way, knowing that our Creator is bending down to listen—knowing we are extravagantly loved and heard—believing that He is inclining toward us. The precious gift of grace is embedded inside us; the whole of who He is is woven into the fabric of who we are. John 1:16 says, "Out of his fullness we have all received grace in place of grace already given." The Amplified version is even more clear:

Out of His fullness [the superabundance of His grace and truth] we have all received grace upon grace [spiritual blessing upon spiritual blessing, favor upon favor, and gift heaped upon gift].

Inside you, who have chosen to move into grace, who have chosen to live there, you have access to this unlimited grace upon grace, favor upon favor, gift upon gift. You get the chocolate factory. You may choose to live inside it, even as it lives inside you. Lean into Him, love Him, as He leans into you. There is truly no better place to be.

PRAYER

Gracious Lord, thank You for leaning toward me and being attentive to my life and who I am. Help me to live a life in gratitude for Your grace. Lord, I deserve nothing You have offered, yet You give freely anyway. Help me to rest in Your leaning and extend that grace to those around me.

QUESTIONS

1. How do you see God's attentiveness and care in your daily life?
2. What things in your life make it difficult to lean back toward God as He leans into you?
3. What are you doing in response to the grace and favor you receive from God?

4. When you think of grace as a space to live rather than an object to grasp, how does that affect your previous ideas and beliefs about grace?

5. What other spaces do we often find ourselves living in rather than grace (examples: perfectionism, comparison, etc.)?

Chapter 5
Redemption
Ephesians 1:7
Teddy Copeland

ONE MAIN THING

When I was assigned the topic of redemption, I couldn't help but recall a Bible class I took in college in the late 1970s. More often than not, the professor came bounding into our classroom singing at the top of his lungs. One of his favorites was the hymn which begins, "Redeemed, how I love to proclaim it! Redeemed by the blood of the Lamb."[1] Both the tune and his manner were infectious, implying, "How could we *not* be overjoyed at the position in which we, as God's children, find ourselves?" And how could we not echo the words of another beloved hymn, this one with the line, "Redeeming love has been my theme, and shall be till I die"?[2] Paul seems to share a similar sentiment with these songwriters when he says in Ephesians 1:7, "In Him we have redemption through His blood, the forgiveness of sins, according to the riches of His grace" (NKJV).

GOING DEEPER

The Oxford English Dictionary says redemption is: "(1) the action of saving or being saved from sin or evil; or (2) the action of gaining or regaining possession of something in exchange for payment or clearing a debt."[3] The biblical concept of redemption combines both of these ideas.

Concerning salvation, we know that when man sinned by eating the forbidden fruit in the garden of Eden, there was a penalty to be paid for his disobedience. According to Romans 3:23, the price for sin is death. But God already had in place a plan to save humanity.

Here's a simple story to illustrate. A king ruled over a mighty kingdom. There was just one problem: An inordinate amount of stealing occurred there on a regular basis. Naturally, the king was concerned, so he decided to take drastic measures. He passed a decree that anyone caught stealing would be punished by having his two eyes put out. Surely, he thought, with such a severe penalty, thieves would think twice before stealing. For a while, things seemed to get better. But then, one day, a servant reported there had been another incident. The thief was brought forth, and, to the king's horror, it was his own son! Thus, he found himself in quite a predicament. In order to be just, he had to follow through with the prescribed punishment. But, as a father, he loved his son and couldn't stand the thought of his being blind. After a great deal of thought, the king came up with a solution. He instructed servants to put out one of the eyes of his son and one of his own eyes. In so doing, justice was served because two eyes were put out, just as he had decreed. But by giving a part of himself, his son's eyesight was spared. That, in a nutshell, is what our heavenly Father—both just and merciful—did for us. He gave a part of Himself (His own Son!) to meet the requirement and spare us from death.

In the pages of the Old Testament, the term "redemption" most frequently refers to what God did in bringing Israel out of Egyptian slavery, saving or delivering them. But other uses of the word, particularly specifications of the law, emphasize the second part of the Oxford definition—the concept of regaining or buying something back. For example, if someone became poor and was forced to sell part of his property, the Lord commanded that his nearest relative could come and redeem what had been sold (Lev 25:25).

A real-life illustration helps me to better understand this aspect of redemption. In 1998, my Uncle Bill and Aunt Mary built their dream house in the country. Six years later, however, they sold it in order to move in with Uncle Bill's brother, my Uncle Delmar. His wife had passed away, and he had no one to care for him. In one of the most unselfish acts I've ever witnessed (and not just because they're relatives!), they put their belongings in storage and centered their lives around him. When he passed in 2011, their plan was to remodel his house, move in their things, and make it their own. But the couple who had bought their property decided it was too far from town, so Bill and Mary were able to buy it back—

to redeem it! That dream house they'd so carefully constructed and still loved became theirs once again.

Sometimes, in music, songs conclude with the same line with which they opened. In God's word, something similar happens. Revelation 22 describes some of the very things we saw at the beginning of time in the garden of Eden in Genesis. It's like we've gone full circle: starting out one way and then, throughout the Bible, trying to get back to where we were, to that perfect communion between God and man before sin created a chasm. That was the whole point of Jesus' death—to redeem us and buy back what was lost, to restore that relationship we were created for in the first place!

Let's consider two instances of redemption in the Bible. The first is found in Ruth. Near the end of the book, just when it seems the tragedy of Ruth's widowhood will be resolved, a conflict arises. Another man—not Boaz, who's been so kind to the young widow—has a prior claim to marry her. At the start of chapter 4, Boaz goes to the city gate where all official business is done. The nearer kinsman comes along, and Boaz lays out the situation. Naomi is giving up what little property she has, and the nearer kinsman can redeem it, so the inheritance will remain in the family. At this point Boaz tells the *go'el* (more on that term in a minute) that Naomi has a daughter-in-law, and, as the kinsman/redeemer, he must take her as his wife and raise up offspring in the name of her dead husband, Mahlon. With that piece of information, the kinsman changes his mind, clearing the path for Boaz.

Notice the requirements for a *go'el*, that term in the OT for "redeemer," one who comes forth to reclaim something. There are three stipulations. He must (1) be near of kin, (2) be able to redeem, and (3) be willing to redeem. The third qualification was where things fell apart for Boaz's rival. He had the capacity to redeem but wasn't willing.

Scriptures show how Jesus qualifies to be our Redeemer. First, there is the kinship (Heb 2:14–15). Second, He has the ability to redeem (Heb 7:25). And then there's the willingness (Mark 10:45). He didn't have to do it. He could have backed out—even as late as in the garden before the soldiers arrived—but He didn't.

A second example of redemption is in the book of Hosea. Hosea's wife deserts him for another. Out of this, he grasps with rare insight the pain in the heart of God when His people forsake and forget Him. This is what makes this story so special—because it is a picture of God's love for us. Hosea finds Gomer, probably on the trading block of an auction, about to be sold as a slave. And he buys her back.

WRAPPING IT UP

Here are three things about redemption that are important to remember.

1. Redemption is personal. In 1975, Raymond Dunn Jr. was born in New York state. At birth, a skull fracture and oxygen deprivation caused severe

impairment. He was blind, mute, and immobile. His twisted body suffered up to ten seizures a day. He had severe allergies that limited him to only one food: a meat-based formula made by Gerber. But in 1985 Gerber stopped making that formula. His mother scoured the country to purchase what stores had in stock, accumulating cases and cases, but in 1990 her supply ran out. In desperation, she appealed to Gerber. Without this food, her son would starve to death! The company listened. In an unprecedented action, volunteers donated hundreds of hours to bring out old equipment, set up production lines, obtain special approval from the USDA, and produce it—all for one special boy. Raymond lived until 1995.[4] That story reminds me that if I had been the only sinner on earth, God still would have sent His Son for me. It's why in my Bible, in John 3:16, I've crossed out the words "the world" and filled in my own name. God's love was such that He gave Jesus for me!

2. Redemption is precious. First Peter 1:19 says we were ransomed with the "precious blood of Christ, as of a lamb without blemish and without spot." What Jesus did is not to be taken lightly. In 2009, the U.S. had already secured their spot for the 2010 World Cup, but they had one game left to play against Costa Rica. The outcome of the game didn't matter for the U.S., but it did for Costa Rica. And it also mattered for another team in the group, Honduras. For Honduras to go

to the World Cup, the U.S. needed to either beat or tie Costa Rica. Things didn't look good, though, because with the game almost over, the U.S. was trailing 1-0. Suddenly, though, an unlikely hero emerged. In the very last seconds, an American, Jonathan Bernstein, scored to tie the game. He became an instant hero in Honduras (a country which hadn't been to the World Cup in decades). The president of the country offered Bernstein an all-expenses-paid trip to a Honduran resort. His image was imposed on the country's currency. His goal was shown repeatedly on TV, and headlines in newspapers read *Honduras te ama* ("Honduras loves you"). They even made soccer jerseys with his name on the back. "He's like our savior," one fan said. "He made seven million people happy."[5] That's overwhelming gratitude, isn't it? It's the kind of gratitude we should feel for our Savior.

3. Redemption is propelling. The word "propel" means to drive, push, or cause to move in a particular direction, typically forward. What should we do in response to what Jesus has done for us? Psalm 107:2 says, "Let the redeemed of the Lord say so, whom He has redeemed from the hand of the enemy." "Has the Lord redeemed you?" the Living Bible asks. "Then speak out!" (Ps 107:2 TLB). May we all have greater courage to speak out about the great redemption that is ours as God's children.

PRAYER

Precious Savior, thank You for being willing to redeem me from all my faults. Help me to remember I could not be saved without Your redeeming blood, and help me to stay grateful and humble in this all of my days.

QUESTIONS

1. Redemption can mean being saved from evil or restoring what was lost. Which of these do you think requires the most grace from God—saving us from our sins or restoring to us the blessings He promised? Why?
2. Have you ever been rescued from disaster (literally or figuratively)? What was it like? How can you rescue others and point them to God at the same time?
3. How would you explain the full, biblical concept of redemption to someone who doesn't know much about the Bible?
4. What can you change in your life right now to demonstrate that you have been redeemed?

Chapter 6

Forgiveness

Ephesians 1:7

Betty Hamblen

ONE MAIN THING

Forgiveness of our sins is an incredible, life-changing blessing.

INTRODUCTION

The God-following Jewish man, Saul, was an accomplice to a murder. He had listened as that upstart Stephen spouted all kinds of crazy ideas about a heretic named Jesus. Stephen certainly deserved punishment in Saul's thinking, and in the thinking of his fellow Jews, who began calling for Stephen's death. Saul determined to help the ones calling for his death. He watched over their garments when they threw them at his feet to be unencumbered as they snatched up heavy rocks, and he watched as they stoned the blasphemer to death. In his opinion, the country needed to be rid of all those followers of Jesus who were talking nonsense. He pledged to do his part in making that happen.

For the next several months, the Jesus-followers shook with fear when they heard the name of Saul. He hauled out of their homes the men and women who talked about a new religion, and he had them sent straight to prison. In telling this story later, Saul said that he persecuted them "to the death" (Acts 22:4 ESV). What Saul did was fully approved by the Jewish rulers, but in God's eyes, he must have been a murderer.

Saul was certainly successful in his pursuit. But, it came to a stunning and sudden halt one fateful day. Saul, traveling with a small company of men, was on his way to Damascus with letters to the synagogues verifying his "right" to rid the city of those outliers of religion. Suddenly, Jesus spoke to him from heaven, and the authority, power, kingship, and light of the Son of God struck him blind. Blind Saul asked who the Lord was. When the Lord told him He was Jesus whom Saul persecuted, Saul had no doubt. This Jesus was the Son of God, and Saul had sinned against Him. The unbeliever became a believer who would spend the rest of his life teaching others about Jesus the Savior.

In the years following that meeting of man and the divine, there must have been many times that Paul, the Greek name that he came to be called, lamented over his past behavior. Perhaps he awoke in the night, heart beating rapidly because of nightmares about those, just like himself now, whom he had roughly persecuted. I wonder if sometimes, as he was teaching about his loving Lord and Master, Paul remembered the serene face of Stephen looking toward heaven as he took his last breath.

What sins he had committed against God's own people, his own people now! What burdens of guilt! What total forgiveness offered by the Savior, for he had been cleansed by the blood of Jesus through baptism!

GOING DEEPER

Paul later spoke about his earlier sins and once even described himself as the "foremost" of sinners (1 Tim 1:15). When such a murderer as Paul talks about forgiveness, we should pay special attention. When he speaks, as he does in Ephesians 1:7, of the spiritual blessings found in Christ and specifically mentions forgiveness of sins, we should "sit up and take notice" because he knows from experience what he is talking about.

Forgiveness is not just a word to someone like that. It is a heart-revealing meeting with Jesus. It is a soul washed clean by the blood of the Savior. It is an unburdening of guilt. It is a path to a new life.

If we read closely the entire story of Saul's conversion (Acts 9) and then think about how we and others find forgiveness in Christ, we find common elements—a pattern, if you will, or at least shared experiences. The pattern seems to have three indisputable elements for those who turn their lives from focusing on worldly pursuits to focusing on following Jesus: recognition, repentance, and reconciliation.

Recognition

Those who pursue a relationship with Jesus first *recognize who He is*. Before Saul met Jesus on that roadway to Damascus, he knew God. He was steeped in religion as a passionate follower of the Jewish law, having been educated by the well-known teacher, Gamaliel. He described himself later as "being zealous for God" (Acts 22:3).

We would perhaps describe him as an upright, godly man. But, he did not know Jesus. Jesus, he thought, was a renegade Jew trying to destroy the millennia-old system of religion and laws given by God Himself.

Saul's up-close and personal meeting with the Christ on that roadway changed his mind in a heartbeat. He was stricken by the blinding light of the Son of God's glory and majesty. When Jesus told Saul who He was, there seemed to be not an iota of doubt in Saul's mind that this was the true One. He never questioned but must have believed immediately that the true Son of God, with all His power and authority, called his name and pointed out his sin. Saul then waited in complete submission as he was told what to do.

Those who become followers of Jesus follow the same path that Saul did. In faith they recognize the absolute and real authority and power that Jesus has over them and over the earth. They recognize the complete love Jesus has for them. Otherwise, they would not believe in Him or choose to submit their lives to Him.

When did you first recognize who Jesus is? Did a co-worker with a Bible introduce you to Him on a work break, or did a spouse who loved you encourage you by teaching about Him? Did you hear a sermon that opened your heart, or were you simply knocked to your knees by life's circumstances and cried out to Him?

Your first meeting with Jesus may or may not have been as dramatic and immediate as Paul's meeting. But, at some point, perhaps after days, weeks, or years, all who will become His children must *recognize who Jesus is.* Son of God. The Lord Jesus Christ. Holy Savior. This recognition brings about another part of the pattern.

By recognizing who Jesus really is, those who understand His glory, majesty, and purity also *recognize who they are* in comparison and are struck by that recognition. The contrast is stunning and stark. Jesus has all authority; they are nothing. Jesus is sinless; they are filled with sin. Jesus is holy; they are unholy. Jesus is as white as snow; they are unclean.

The great prophet Isaiah certainly recognized who he was in contrast to the glorious God he saw in a vision. The God he saw was seated on a throne being worshipped by seraphim who extolled His glory and His holiness. In the presence of that holiness and splendor of God, Isaiah immediately saw his own sinful, weak character. He declared, "I am lost; for I am a man of unclean lips, and I dwell in the midst of a people of unclean lips" (Isa 6:5).

Saul had the same experience. The blinding splendor and glory of Jesus not only struck Saul's eyesight, but it also struck his soul. He could not eat nor drink for three days afterward but was in fervent prayer.

I wonder about that time. Did he beg God for forgiveness for the sins he had committed against Him? Did he name each one that he remembered? Did sorrow strike his soul as the faces of those people he had sent to prison or to death flooded his memory? Surely, he prayed for the strength he would need to leave his old way of life and become a new man of Christ, for he did just that without looking back.

Repentance

When we talk about this subject, we must mention the difficulty that is inherent in repentance. Sometimes it is a killer that keeps many from having those sins washed away. Do you know what this difficulty is? It is pride. Repentance requires humility, the absence of pride.

Every person has a central core that is all about self, and the steel rod that seems to keep that core intact is pride. All of us have pride of self, some more than others. Having the ability to put pride aside and humble oneself to admit "I am nothing but a sinner, and I need to be cleansed from those sins" is too hard for some people, but it is absolutely essential to become a child of God.

Saul had every reason to be proud. He was educated by a renowned teacher. He had Roman citizenship and was brought up in Jerusalem, the great city of David. He was respected enough by the Jewish religious leaders that they granted his requests to find and persecute members of the Way, and Saul was excellent at that job.

But when Jesus showed Saul who he really was, there was left no pride in self or in his accomplishments. He spent three complete days doing nothing but praying to God, and when Ananias came to him, telling him to "rise and be baptized and wash away your sins, calling on his name" (Acts 22:16), there was no hesitation. He was a complete sinner who needed the forgiveness that only Jesus could give.

Repentance calls for a turning away from former, worldly things and turning toward the things of Jesus. Saul did just that without ever looking back, and his life was never the same again.

In his letter to the Philippians, he recounted all the reasons for the pride that he had before he became a Christian. Then he penned these words: "For his sake I have suffered the loss of all things and count them as rubbish, in order that I may gain Christ" (Phil 3:8). He explained in the next verse that he did not gain righteousness of his own doing but "the righteousness from God that depends on faith" (Phil 3:9). Saul had been forgiven of his sins against God and had gained a righteousness that was not one he worked for, but one that came by his faith in Jesus Christ.

Reconciliation

The third part of the pattern is all about a relationship, a restored relationship. We are God's from the beginning of life. He gives us our life. He breathes into our nostrils our very breath, but at some point after childhood, our sins separate us from the Most Holy One.

Since God has complete holiness, we, who are unholy and sinful, can have no relationship with Him. But, as Paul noted, "while we were enemies we were reconciled to God by the death of his Son," and we have "been justified by his blood" (Rom 5:9–10).

The forgiveness of our sins, through the sacrifice of the sinless and holy Jesus, washes us clean and restores the relationship between Father and child. His forgiveness means we can walk with Him through the Word, talk with Him about our lives, praise Him, thank Him for His grace and mercy, repent of current sins, and be washed clean daily. Because we have obeyed Him and are forgiven, we are children in His family, holy ones now. The forgiven ones.

WRAPPING IT UP

Forgiveness is so precious and life-giving that God expects something from the forgiven. Read Mark 11:25–26; Luke 6:37; 11:4; 17:3–4. God's expectation is clear. He asks us to forgive those who sin against us. Whether they apologize or not is immaterial. After all, they have broken His laws, not ours. He is the lawmaker; we are not. Vengeance is His, not ours (Rom 12:19).

Paul knew something about forgiving someone whom he felt had wronged him. When he and Barnabas left on their first missionary journey, the young man John Mark assisted them. However, well before they were finished teaching and preaching in all the places they had determined, Mark left them and went back home.

Later, after they themselves had returned to Jerusalem and then settled in Antioch, Paul wanted to revisit all the brothers and sisters they had taught on their first journey. Barnabas was all for it but wanted to take John Mark with them. Paul decidedly did not. The young man had abandoned them and the work. Paul and Barnabas separated their work, and Barnabas took John Mark with him to Cyprus.

Perhaps Barnabas mentored John Mark and helped him to grow up a little. Perhaps Mark gained a little more experience in work and dedication as he helped Barnabas to spread the word of God. And perhaps Paul grew also.

Years later, when Paul was imprisoned in Rome, he wrote a second letter to Timothy, a young man he had mentored as they worked in various cities to spread the gospel. Paul called Timothy his "true child in the faith" (1 Tim 1:2). As he was writing the letter, perhaps another young man from his past came to mind.

Inviting Timothy to come and see him soon, Paul also included this instruction: "Get Mark and bring him with you, for he is very useful to me for ministry" (2 Tim 4:11). Through the years, Paul had absorbed well the lessons and character of God. Through his own experience, he was well-acquainted with forgiveness and its redemptive nature. Remembering his own need for forgiveness, he passed it on to another.

Forgiveness. To be unburdened by sin. To have guilt and shame lifted. To mend a relationship. To be reconciled with God and one another.

Forgiveness! What a blessing!

PRAYER

Dear Lord, thank You for the ability to see who You are, to see through You what I lack, and to come to You to be made whole. Help me to lay aside my pride so that I may be reconciled to and in relationship with You. Your forgiveness is greater than my sin, and I will forever be grateful.

QUESTIONS

1. How does Paul's backstory make his teaching on forgiveness so powerful?
2. Can you identify the time in your life when you recognized Jesus, repented, and were reconciled to God?

3. Where are you currently falling short of the perfection of Jesus? For what sins do you currently need the blessing of forgiveness?

4. How does forgiveness unburden us? Can you think of a personal relationship that was unburdened by forgiveness?

Chapter 7

Knowledge

Ephesians 1:9, 17

Cathy Turner

ONE MAIN THING

God's book is so amazing! In what other book can you study on a couple of words forever and still never finish—words such as "In the beginning..." (Gen 1:1 NKJV), "The Lord is..." (Ps 23:1), or those in our study here in Ephesians 1, "In Him"? In Ephesians 1, some form of "in Him" appears at least ten times. We are reminded that "in Him" are all spiritual blessings, redemption, adoption, and inheritance, and "in Him" we should put our trust. But we can't come to know any of this if we don't read Ephesians. We won't know how to apply these comforts wisely if we don't take this knowledge in and add it to our faith and love for Jesus Christ. Knowledge carries the power of the gospel.

What I am saying on one level is very simple—knowledge is essential. Without knowledge you cannot understand something. I would not know how to put words on this page if I had not learned. I know nothing much about Uruguay because I have not studied it. You know how to use scissors because someone showed you, and you practiced. We can know of God without His book, says Romans 1:20: "For since the creation of the world His invisible attributes are clearly seen, being understood by the things that are made, even His eternal power and Godhead, so that they are without excuse." Yes, we can know of Him; but to know Him intimately, to be "partakers of the divine nature" (2 Pet 1:4), we have to have knowledge.

In Paul's opening remarks to the saints who were in Ephesus and whom he deemed faithful, he shares sweet thoughts that he has prayed for them. In verses 17–18, Paul prays "that the God of our Lord Jesus Christ, the Father of glory, may give to you the spirit of wisdom and revelation in the knowledge of Him, the eyes of your understanding being enlightened" (Eph 1:17–18). In this chapter of Scripture, where Paul reiterates what blessings can be found "in Christ," he says that in the knowledge of Him, wisdom, revelation, understanding, and enlightenment can be found. Truly, knowledge of Christ is power.

Proverbs 1:7 says, "The fear of the Lord is the beginning of knowledge, but fools despise wisdom and instruction." Respect for God begins with knowledge. God wishes for us to pursue knowledge of Him. Proverbs 22:17 says, "Apply your heart to my knowledge," and 2 Peter 1:5 says, "Add to your faith virtue, to virtue knowledge." We are talking about spiritual knowledge here, not carnal. Paul warns Timothy, "O Timothy! Guard what was committed to your trust, avoiding the profane and idle babblings and contradictions of what is falsely called knowledge— by professing it some have strayed concerning the faith" (1 Tim 6:20-21). Ecclesiastes 2:26 states, "For God gives wisdom and knowledge and joy to a man who is good in His sight." "God-given things to know" are what Paul is discussing with the Ephesians. The Ephesians have already been described as obedient believers: "In Him you also trusted, after you heard the word of truth, the gospel of your salvation; in whom also, having believed, you were sealed with the Holy Spirit of promise, who is the guarantee of our inheritance" (Eph 1:13-14).

GOING DEEPER

A Mindset for Wisdom

Like the Ephesians, we, who have heard, trusted, and believed in the Lord and His gospel, must move forward, deeper into the knowledge that God has given and that the Holy Spirit has laid out, protected, and assured. To receive the joy and wisdom that God's knowledge brings, we must have a mindset, a spirit ready to pursue and receive wisdom and revelation. This desire to know more comes from the hidden woman of the heart. God rewards that spirit by giving wisdom, as Ecclesiastes 2:26 states. Paul does not pray for God to give the Ephesians wisdom directly; he prays that God will bolster the desire (spirit) of the Ephesians for wisdom. Do you want to be wise?

Have you undoubtingly asked for wisdom (Jas 1:5)? Do you have the mindset to pursue wisdom? Do you study and meditate on the word so that God and His Spirit can touch your heart and help you to see?

Remember Job? Listen to his words, in Job 42:1–6, after he had gone deeper with God:

> Then Job answered the Lord and said: "I know that You can do everything, and that no purpose of Yours can be withheld from You. You asked, 'Who is this who hides counsel without knowledge?' Therefore I have uttered what I did not understand, things too wonderful for me, which I did not know. Listen, please, and let me speak; You said, 'I will question you, and you shall answer Me.' I have heard of You by the hearing of the ear, but now my eye sees You. Therefore I abhor myself, and repent in dust and ashes."

Job's interaction with God had deepened his knowledge of God. He no longer just knew of God; he knew God. He had heard His words, but now his eyes of understanding were opened. He was humbled. He submitted. Job repented of his self-attitude. Once we have understanding of God's words, the putting away of self is the genuine reaction. Submission is necessary. Job had gained knowledge, and with it came understanding. Knowledge and understanding precede wisdom. Knowing God is wisdom, and wisdom gives life. Ecclesiastes 7:12

says, "But the excellence of knowledge is that wisdom gives life to those who have it."

Wisdom says:

> Listen, for I will speak of excellent things, and from the opening of my lips will come right things; for my mouth will speak truth. ... All the words of my mouth are with righteousness. ... They are all plain to him who understands, and right to those who find knowledge. ... For wisdom is better than rubies, and all the things one may desire cannot be compared with her. (Prov 8:6-11)

She adds, "Counsel is mine, and sound wisdom; I am understanding, I have strength. ... I love those who love me, and those who seek me diligently will find me." (Prov 8:14, 17)

Enlightenment

> The LORD possessed me [wisdom] at the beginning of His way ... from the beginning, before there was ever an earth. ... Before the hills, I was brought forth; ... When He prepared the heavens, I was there. ... I was beside Him as a master craftsman; and I was daily His delight, rejoicing always before Him (Prov 8:22-23, 25, 27, 30).

Wisdom is to be respected and desired. It is understanding, strength, life, and lasts forever. Grab hold! It's available! God doesn't leave us in the dark. He states and restates and makes everything clear, so that our eyes of understanding will be enlightened. As Job did, we have to open our eyes, our hearts, so that we can see. In John 14:15–17, Christ said:

> If you love Me, keep My commandments. And I will pray the Father, and He will give you another Helper, that He may abide with you forever [which includes now!]—the Spirit of truth, whom the world cannot receive, because it neither sees Him nor knows Him; but you know Him, for He dwells with you and will be in you.

And Christ continues in verse 23: "If anyone loves Me, he will keep My word; and My Father will love him, and We will come to him and make Our home with him" (John 14:23). The Godhead will make a home with us if we keep the word. Wow! Just wow! The company of God comes with knowledge.

How can we keep the word if we don't know it? How can we not sin if we don't know God (1 Cor 15:34)? How can we put on the new man if we have no knowledge (Col 3:10)? How can we reach others, warn our sister-friends, or teach our children if we are not filled with all knowledge (Rom 15:14)? Paul prays for faithful saints to have knowledge because it is powerful! We are the light! God wants us to have knowledge of what He has worked through Christ so that His church will be full:

> That the Father of glory may give to you the spirit of wisdom and revelation in the knowledge of Him, the eyes of your understanding being enlightened; that you may know what is the hope of His calling, what are the riches of the glory of His inheritance in the saints, and what is the exceeding greatness of His power toward us who believe, according to the working of His mighty power which He worked in Christ when He raised Him from the dead and seated Him at His right hand in the heavenly places, far above all principality and power and might and dominion, and every name that is named, not only in this age but also in that which is to come. And He put all things under His feet, and gave Him to be head over all things to the church, which is His body, the fullness of Him who fills all in all. (Eph 1:17–23)

Amen to the knowledge of Him. We have got to love His book!

WRAPPING IT UP

In conclusion, in the fullness of Him, the church has to share our knowledge of Him. We must teach. We can teach only what we know. Closing with example and application, I share my *Cat and Kids* column entitled "Teach."[1]

For Christ's sake, desire knowledge so that you can teach.

"TEACH"

The other evening, I received the sweetest text. It was an audio message, and the caption read, "Singing ourselves to sleep," with a heart icon. It was our daughter and our four-year-old granddaughter softly singing "The Magnificat," composed by Randy Gill. What simple sweetness their voices were. I wish you could have heard it.

> My soul magnifies the Lord
> My spirit rejoices in God my Savior
> My soul magnifies the Lord
> My spirit rejoices in God.[2]

The two of them were confidently singing their parts—harmonizing in places. Quietly calming their own hearts.

Truly a little tear came to my eye—for many reasons. I wish that I could have been there, but mostly I was thankful. Thankful that our daughter is teaching our granddaughter to sing, and how to sing. I'm so thankful that our children ran into people in their lives who taught them how to sing. Lora's alto voice is strong, smooth, and beautiful, and she is teaching Ruby how to sing. But more importantly, she is teaching her to sing. Music is a thread that sews us together. Music is a part of our family culture.

And then a day or two later, I stepped into our den to see our son, Randall, sitting on the sofa strumming his ukulele with his three-year-old daughter sitting on his feet strumming her mini wooden guitar with six strings. Oh, the music they were making! I wish you could have heard it. I'm sure his song had a title, but I couldn't make it out because Mica was drowning him out. They both had the sweetest smiles on their faces, and plain ole happiness in their hearts.

One of my favorite mama moments was a few years ago on Mother's Day. Our son, Garrett, stood up and sang Boyz II Men's "A Song for Mama" to me right in the restaurant at the table where we were having Sunday dinner. He sang unabashedly and lovingly. All of the mamas in our section of the restaurant loved it. I cried. He had no fear—only voice and feeling. He was in his comfort zone. I didn't teach him how to sing, but I/we taught him to love music—Motown and musicals, hymns and Hogan. We passed it to him. The love of music was passed to us.

We teach what we know, you know. That's one reason that families have long lines of singers or teachers or doctors in their midst. We do what we do in front of our children. We talk about it at the dinner table and teach it when we don't know we are teaching. Natural. This is one of the plights of the disadvantaged—no natural training of higher ideology, processes, or tactics. No examples. We teach what we know. Luckily, some people choose to mentor, to open doors, to share.

My grandbabies are blessed, being taught by parents who have taken in many good teachings. Our children are such good parents—i.e., teaching "The Magnificat" as a lullaby. As I listen to our granddaughter singing those words with her mom (and I have listened several times), I know that she has been taught what the words "magnifies" and "rejoice" mean. I imagine that conversation. I wish I could have heard it. It would have been music to my ears. Teach (Deut 6:4-9).

PRAYER

God of truth, help me never to stop in my pursuit of knowledge inspired by You. Help me to stay hungry for Your word and joyful in the pursuit. Give me the strength to lay aside my pride, so I can fully receive the wisdom You offer from above.

QUESTIONS

1. How does looking at knowledge as a blessing from God dispel pride?
2. How have you leaned on your own understanding in the past? How did that affect your faith?
3. What are some of the ways you have pursued godly knowledge today? This week? This year? Is that a priority in Your life?
4. Second Peter 1:5 urges us to add virtue to our faith and knowledge to our virtue. Why are faith and virtue listed as precursors to knowledge?

Chapter 8
Inheritance

Ephesians 1:11, 14, 18

Keli Brothers

ONE MAIN THING

Hearing the word "inheritance" naturally invokes at least one of two thoughts: Something is about to be gained and/or something has just been lost. The concept of inheritance is by no means new or newly understood. Although it has a long history, it is not often openly discussed, as it carries its own form of taboo. Much like race and politics, inheritance is not considered appropriate for conversation at the dinner table—that is, until it is discussed in a spiritual context. However, the rudimentary elements of inheritance are essential to understanding the spiritual implications.

So, what does inheritance mean? The basic definition of inheritance involves the receipt of something from a predecessor of familial or relational ties upon said predecessor's death. Therein lies the taboo of the topic: Because of its direct association with death, the discussion of inheritance is often one held in privacy. This is also part of the great affront of the prodigal son to his father in asking for his inheritance not only early, but also before his older brother (Luke 15:11–32). In reviewing the first chapter of Ephesians, one can see the beauty of the concept of spiritual inheritance and learn why this type of inheritance is one that should be spoken of openly and frequently.

INTRODUCTION

An important legal element of the definition of inheritance is the acknowledgement that the person leaving the inheritance knows the person inheriting. Most often it is a close relative, but there are many instances of heirs who are distant relatives, friends, or even business partners. The common denominator is that the inheritor must be known to the person leaving the inheritance. Inheritance is rarely left to a stranger.

If we are viewing Scripture from the context of Jewish tradition, inheritance belonged to the firstborn son.[1] Second sons traditionally received a verbal blessing by the father and some minor financial assistance, but were mostly left at the mercy of their elder brother when the father passed away. The first son was raised with the expectation that one day he would inherit the established estate of the father. He would have been trained on its maintenance to ensure its perpetuity along with that of the family bloodline. Also, the first son would have worked closely with the father, learning from him and receiving correction as the father slowly began delegating various aspects of the estate to the son. There was a lot of responsibility associated with such an inheritance.[2]

Recent history shows that provisions in the Jewish tradition have changed to allow for various distributions of estates amongst siblings; new provisions do not limit the inheritance to first sons or only sons, but also include daughters.[3] Thus, by default of being a person's child, one has an opportunity to inherit.

Legally, there are five basic steps in the process of obtaining one's inheritance:

1. First, there is the establishment of a will.
2. Then comes the identification of beneficiaries.
3. Third is the death of the person leaving the inheritance.
4. Debts are settled.
5. Finally, assets are transferred.

Through the first chapter of Ephesians, one can see how Christ followed not only Jewish tradition, but legal tradition. Ephesians 1:11 states, "In Him also we have obtained an inheritance, being predestined according to the purpose of Him who works all things according to the counsel of His *will*." (NJKV). Just a few verses prior, the reader was informed of the adoption of Christians as sons and daughters of God, making them siblings of the first Son, Christ (Eph 1:5). So, because Christians are considered via adoption to be sons and daughters, there is an opportunity to inherit, just like in modern Jewish tradition. Scripture clearly indicates that Christ wants all to inherit: "The Lord is not slack concerning His promise, as some count slackness, but is longsuffering toward us, not *willing* that any should perish but that *all* should come to repentance" (2 Pet 3:9).

Why is this significant? The terms "heir" and "beneficiary" are not fully interchangeable, as an heir is a beneficiary, but a beneficiary does not have to be an heir. The term "heir" automatically assumes a level of kinship or blood relation that can be proven. A beneficiary is someone specifically chosen to receive all or a portion of an inheritance. An heir is assumed the right of inheritance; a beneficiary must directly be named by the person leaving the inheritance.[4] In the absence of a will specifying beneficiaries, assets default to the living heirs. However, with a beneficiary statement, an estate can be divided between heirs and beneficiaries as delegated by the one leaving the inheritance. Therein lies the significance—believers are not only heirs, but we are also listed as beneficiaries, chosen to be a part of God's own family. Our Father in Heaven chose all, and those who also choose Him will obtain an inheritance called eternity. It is His will (step 1 above), and He has listed all who repent as His beneficiaries (step 2).

In His death, burial, and resurrection, Christ went on to follow the third, fourth, and fifth steps of the legal inheritance process. Ephesians 1:13–14 states, "You were sealed with the Holy Spirit of promise, who is the guarantee [down payment/earnest] of our inheritance until the redemption of the purchased possession, to the praise of His glory." When Christ died (step 3), He settled the debts of sin (step 4) and began the process of the transfer of assets to the beneficiaries (step 5). He left Christians with the initial components of the immeasurable inheritance found in salvation, including a relationship with and guidance toward the Father in Heaven.

GOING DEEPER

Again, when the word "inheritance" is heard, one most often acknowledges two truths: Something has been lost, and something will be gained. Also, in the general operation of inheritance, the "lost" portion comes first. A self-assessment for Christians will show that there were a number of losses necessary for our inheritance to be gained.

One of the primary losses was us, humanity. We were lost in our sin. We needed saving and had proven more than once our inability to "save ourselves." This led to the next necessary loss: The Son left the direct presence of God the Father to come to earth (John 3:16; 6:38–40). The third loss is one that was the most significant: the loss of the Savior's life (temporarily, praise God!). Again, for inheritance to be inheritance, a loss of such a kind is imperative. The law requires that there be a death and proof thereof. Christ fulfilled this requirement on the cross, and the soldiers ensured His death by piercing His side (John 19:34). However, what no attorney could have prepared for was that there would be a resurrection. There is nothing stating that the one leaving an inheritance must "remain dead," only that said person must die.

So, if this is what was lost, what was gained?

> May [God] give to you the spirit of wisdom and revelation in the knowledge of Him, the eyes of your understanding being enlightened; that you may know what is the hope of His calling, what are the riches of the glory of His inheritance in the saints. (Eph 1:17–18)

We often think of inheritance as monetary gain, but when thinking of spiritual inheritance, one must think of things more significant than monetary gain. People can inherit all manner of things—some positive, some stressful, some not so great. There is genetic inheritance: facial features, hair color, height, complexion, illnesses, and even more recently discovered, stored trauma.[5] There is financial inheritance: estates, vehicles, trusts, businesses, and debts. There is social inheritance: "A good name is to be chosen rather than great riches, loving favor rather than silver and gold" (Prov 22:1; cf. Eccl 7:1). As discussed earlier, being an inheritor comes with a level of responsibility to monitor, maintain the good, and remove that which is not desirable.

One of the first things inherited was direct access to the Father. In the time between expulsion from Eden to the death, burial, and resurrection of Christ, there was not direct access to the Father in heaven. One could go to the temple to pray and worship; however, to atone for sin one had to go through the priests, who petitioned on one's behalf via sacrifices. Furthermore, the priests had access to the "holy of holies" (the closest place to the presence of God the Father) only once annually. However, upon the death of Christ, the veil to the holy of holies was torn, indicating that access was open to all, not just high priest. "Then the veil of the temple was torn in two from top to bottom" (Mark 15:38). There was no longer waiting for the Day of Atonement for the high priest to go in and (maybe) return having pardoned one's sins.

There is great accountability in having direct access to the Father, as evidenced by the high priests' having a rope tied to them in order to be pulled out of the holy of holies in the event of their passing out or dying from the mere presence of the Father.[6] It is no small gift, no small thing; and Christ serves as a buffer, our very own rope to pull us to the safety of repentance when needed (1 Tim 2:5).

Another initial piece inherited from Christ was help/guidance in the form of the Holy Spirit. "Nevertheless I tell you the truth. It is to your advantage that I go away; for if I do not go away, the Helper will not come to you; but if I depart, I will send Him to you"

(John 16:7). This not only shows again the necessity of the loss, but also provides the hope of help.

Salvation. Reconciliation. This is the one most people immediately consider when thinking about spiritual inheritance, and no doubt what you have been waiting to read about in this chapter. The blessing of inheriting salvation was the purpose of Christ, as He served as the embodiment of forgiveness and reconciliation (Acts 4:12; Isa 53:4–5).

> Now all things are of God, who has reconciled us to Himself through Jesus Christ, and has given us the ministry of reconciliation, that is, that God was in Christ reconciling the world to Himself, not imputing their trespasses to them, and has committed to us the word of reconciliation. (2 Cor 5:18–19)

This is the key to freedom.

Now there is direct access, there is reconciliation, and the Holy Spirit dwells within believers. This provides a new opportunity to have relationships close in resemblance to those in the beginning in Eden. Healthy relationships require reciprocity. Reciprocity means equal effort on both sides.[7] Of course, humans can only do so much, but there have been a few reminders of how to go about this building and maintaining of a relationship with the Father. Second Timothy 2:15, Matthew 6:33, and Proverbs 3:5–6 are a few examples.

In spending time with and studying the Word of God, one develops a connection with the Holy Spirit. The Spirit provides a sword of protection that can cut down the shrubbery of confusion experienced in life, thus serving as a guide clearing a path (cf. 2 Tim 2:15; Eph 6:17). Seeking the kingdom of God and His righteousness requires willingness to change. In healthy relationships, compromise is essential. Being willing to change that which negatively impacts the other person or people is healthy and necessary. Trust is the basic foundation of a relationship. It is rare that people blindly trust unknown people. Trust requires more than acquaintance. Trust takes time to build. Trusting someone means you know that person well enough to believe the person is trustworthy. Remember, it is important that the one providing the inheritance *knows* the inheritor (Prov 3:5-6; Matt 7:21-23).

Something not often discussed is the fact that several responsibilities are inherited along with salvation. One such responsibility is being the bearer of a new, good name, "that the name of our Lord Jesus Christ may be glorified in you, and you in Him, according to the grace of our God and the Lord Jesus Christ" (2 Thess 1:12). In the words of Jesus,

> He who overcomes shall be clothed in white garments, and I will not blot out his name from the Book of Life; but I will confess his name before My Father and before His angels. ... He who overcomes, I will make him a pillar in the temple

of My God, and he shall go out no more. I will write on him the name of My God and the name of the city of My God, the New Jerusalem, which comes down out of heaven from My God. And I will write on him My new name. (Rev 3:5, 12)

As bearers of His name, we have a responsibility to represent Him well. In times of war there are flagbearers with the charge, and these flags bear the name of the king being served. Believers become like this flag, bearing the name of the Christ for all to see.

We have a new function with our spiritual inheritance as well: ambassadorship. This is the daily challenge and task of all those who are believers in Christ:

Now then, we are ambassadors for Christ, as though God were pleading through us: we implore you on Christ's behalf, be reconciled to God. For He made Him who knew no sin to be sin for us, that we might become the righteousness of God in Him. (2 Cor 5:20-21)

There is an inherited responsibility to spread the gospel, to be Christ in the earth, and to remember that everywhere a believer goes the name of God goes as well.

What an honor has been bestowed upon believers! We are not only welcomed into the family, but provided for, with debts reconciled, and encouraged to share the inheritance with others, as there is a surplus to be given.

The blessings of spiritual inheritance that have been gained by faith are not easily numbered, and the inheritance of eternity is truly immeasurable.

WRAPPING IT UP

Not unlike Jewish first sons of the Old Testament, believers are considered sons and daughters of the Father. As such, believers would benefit from living with the expectation of inheriting the established estate of the Father. Believers should train on the maintenance of the body of Christ (study and show yourself approved [2 Tim 2:15]) to ensure its perpetuity and increase the family bloodline.

How do we do this?

Believers should work closely with the Father, learn from Him, and take correction from Him, as He delegates responsibilities and spiritual gifts according to the measures of faith inherited (Rom 12:3-8). The fullness of the responsibility of inheritance is obtained through building and maintaining a relationship with the heavenly Father, living as Christ did, walking in the path provided by Christ, and showing others the benefit of the path by serving with humility and grace. Believers must be willing to discuss the concept of spiritual inheritance at the dinner table, the coffee shop, or the grocery store and do just the same in taking the message to the destitute, imprisoned, hospitalized, and those deemed unreachable.

Now this is left with you: Having received your inheritance and an understanding of the weight it holds, being more than silver and gold (indeed immeasurable), may you live with the joy, peace, and faith expressed in being chosen and take hold the responsibilities of inheritance with boldness.

PRAYER

O God, my portion, thank You for bringing me into Your family so that I may take part in Your immeasurable inheritance. Help me to understand that, as Your adopted heir, I should act in ways befitting one who is called Your daughter.

QUESTIONS

1. In what way is our inheritance something we experience in the present as well as the future?
2. Where is the Father trying to guide you, and what is stopping you from following Him?
3. The song "Mansion over the Hilltop" talks about wanting a luxurious mansion in heaven. Is that greedy? What should our attitude be toward our heavenly reward?
4. Besides salvation, what is the most valuable thing God has already given you?

Chapter 9

Holy Spirit

Ephesians 1:13–14

Rosemary Snodgrass

ONE MAIN THING

In the mid-1970s, a New York attorney appeared on the front porch of a farmhouse in Athens, Alabama. The lawyer came to confirm the identity of a recipient of a large sum of money from a will probated in the state of New York. The recipient, the wife of my father's cousin, had no idea that she was related to one of the founders of the Xerox Corporation, nor that the founder had died. The farmer and his wife had been totally unaware that soon they would receive a very large sum of money. Later, when some family members asked the farmer what he was going to do with several million dollars, he said, "I think I'll buy a new tractor."

Christians have an inheritance coming too, but we've been told it is coming. Paul explains to the readers of Ephesians how God has made this inheritance available to us and how He gives us assurance of this blessing in

Christ. God the Father, God the Son, and God the Spirit, working in unison, have told us the conditions of the will, and they have promised to deliver. We have been chosen, adopted, redeemed, and freed from blame in order to receive this bountiful blessing, and the Holy Spirit has been given to us as a guarantee of this inheritance.

> In him you also, when you heard the word of truth, the gospel of your salvation, and believed in him, were sealed with the promised Holy Spirit, who is the guarantee of our inheritance until we acquire possession of it, to the praise of his glory. (Eph 1:13–14 ESV)

GOING DEEPER

In the first chapter of Ephesians, Paul lays out how the Trinity works together to accomplish great things for us. Their unity of purpose is evident in Their plan to prepare us and qualify us to receive these blessings in Christ.[1] Verse 3 states, "Blessed be the God and Father of our Lord Jesus Christ, who has blessed us in Christ with every spiritual blessing in the heavenly places" (Eph 1:3). God's desire to bless us is truly amazing. Paul opens this letter by praising God because He the creator, the omnipotent, omniscient God of the universe who is willing to love us and bless us. He was willing to send His Son from heaven to earth so that we could be His children also. His Son introduced us to this loving, generous Father in the Sermon on the Mount: "If you then, who are evil, know how to give good gifts to your children, how much more will your Father who is in heaven give good things to those who ask him!" (Matt 7:11).

These good gifts which God has planned for us are not material possessions. They do not rust, nor can a thief steal them (Matt 6:19). Even a downturn in the stock market has no impact on these treasures. These are spiritual blessings. In 1 Corinthians 2:9, Paul reminds us of words written by Isaiah about the inheritance coming to those who love God: "No eye has seen, nor ear heard, nor the heart of man imagined, what God has prepared for those who love him." These gifts will be found in "heavenly places" (Eph 1:3). As Paul identifies in the book of Ephesians (1:3, 20; 2:6; 3:11), they are "in Christ," and they are eternal. Christ's role in providing this inheritance is clear. It is through the willing sacrifice of Jesus Christ that we have forgiveness of sins. Verses 7–12 of Ephesians chapter 1 enlighten us to the fact that because of the payment Christ made on the cross, we can have redemption.[2] Our inheritance is not just the bare necessities.

If you are familiar with the Harry Potter series, you know that, after Harry's parents were murdered, he was sent to live with a cruel aunt and uncle. They barely provided for him. He had to sleep in a closet under the stairway, he wore hand-me-down clothes from his overweight older cousin, and Harry was given meager amounts of food to eat. When he "became of age" at eleven years old, he learned that his parents had left him a vault full of gold to provide for his needs. As you might expect of an eleven-year-old, one of his first unsupervised purchases was a large supply of candy and snacks for himself and a friend. Often, as recipients of the wonderful inheritance of God's grace "which he lavished upon us" (Eph 1:8), we show no more understanding of the magnitude of this gift than Harry or my father's cousin showed of their inheritances. Paul shows great understanding of this gift found in Christ:

> But whatever gain I had, I counted as loss for the
> sake of Christ. Indeed, I count everything as loss
> because of the surpassing worth of knowing
> Christ Jesus my Lord. For his sake I have suffered
> the loss of all things and count them as rubbish,
> in order that I may gain Christ. (Phil 3:7-8)

Many of us have enjoyed the movie *Toy Story*. There is an illustration from that movie that has been repeated in many sermons and Bible lessons to help us understand the role of the Holy Spirit in giving us confidence that we have been given, and will continue to receive, our blessings in Christ. The boy, Andy, has written his name on the sole of the boot of his favorite toy, a cowboy named Woody. Andy has many other toys, but as Andy's birthday approaches, there is great anxiety among them over how the new toys from the birthday party will change the status of the old toys in the toy chest. The toys are concerned that Andy will push them aside because he prefers his new toys. The cowboy Woody looks at the childish scrawl of "Andy" on his boot for reassurance that he belongs to Andy and that his relationship with the boy is strong and reliable. The Holy Spirit is that same reassurance for us, that we belong to God. God has given us the Holy Spirit as His mark on us and the promise of more blessings to come.

Various versions of the Bible use different words or phrases in Ephesians 1:13–14 to describe what the Holy Spirit does for us to give us the assurance that we are being blessed now and we will receive even greater blessings in the future. "In him you ... were *sealed* with the promised Holy Spirit, who is the *guarantee* ..." (ESV) are the words we read. Let's examine a couple of these words. "Sealed" (Greek: *sphragizo*) is defined in *The New Strong's Expanded Exhaustive Concordance of the Bible* as "to *stamp* (with a signet or private mark)."[3] The phrase is translated as "marked in him with a seal" (NIV), "signed, sealed, and delivered" (MSG), or "put his special mark on you" (ERV). This seal, the Holy Spirit, is the mark or indicator that we are heirs. Paul uses similar language when writing to the church in Corinth: "And it is God who establishes us with you in Christ, and has anointed us, and who has also put his seal on us and given us his Spirit in our hearts as a guarantee" (2 Cor 1:21–22). This sealing with the Holy Spirit shows ownership by God and an ongoing relationship between the recipient and God, with a "guarantee" of more blessings to come.

This word "guarantee" used in the ESV is much like the word "sealed" translated in different ways in other versions of the Bible. "Guarantee" (Greek: *arrhabon*), according to *Strong's*, means "a *pledge*" that is "part of the purchase-money or property given in advance as *security* for the rest:—earnest."[4] Various versions of the Bible interpret the phrase as "given as a pledge" (NASB1995), "a deposit guaranteeing" (NIV), or "the first payment" (ERV). This guarantee/pledge/deposit gives us confidence that God will deliver on His promise. In Paul D. Weaver's *Surveying the Pauline Epistles*, we read, "The Holy Spirit's presence in the life of the believer is the assurance that God will finish what He has started, resulting in the believer being taken home to heaven one day."[5]

We can have confidence that God will keep His promise. As we read through the Bible, we see again and again how God made and kept promises to His people. He put a rainbow in the sky as a symbol of His promise to Noah never to destroy the world with a flood again. He promised Abraham to make him the father of a great nation, and, in spite of Abraham's failed attempt to help God keep His promise, God was faithful to His word. God's promise to Abraham was renewed to his descendants, Isaac and Jacob. After returning to the promised land from Egypt, the Israelites lived a roller coaster relationship with God. David was told by God through the prophet Nathan, "Your house and your kingdom shall be made sure forever before me. Your throne shall be established forever" (2 Sam 7:16). David prayed to Yahweh in response to this promise:

And now, O Lord God, you are God, and your words are true, and you have promised this good thing to your servant. Now therefore may it please you to bless the house of your servant, so that it may continue forever before you. For you, O Lord God, have spoken, and with your blessing shall the house of your servant be blessed forever. (2 Sam 7:28–29)

David, described as a man after God's own heart, did not live a sin-free life and recognized there would be consequences for failure to follow God. Following his sin with Bathsheba, he prayed, "Cast me not away from your presence, and take not your Holy Spirit from me" (Ps 51:11). Later, when Solomon, David's son, ascended to the throne and built the temple for the worship of Yahweh, the promise made to David was repeated to Solomon. God offered further explanation to Solomon:

But if you turn aside from following me, you or your children, and do not keep my commandments and my statutes that I have set before you, but go and serve other gods and worship them, then I will cut off Israel from the land that I have given them. (1 Kgs 9:6–7)

In Solomon's later years, he did just as God had told him NOT to do. He was led away by his foreign wives to worship idols. Over the next nine-hundred-plus years, Israel sometimes followed the path to a blessed relationship with Yahweh, but at other times they rejected Yahweh and worshiped idols. Because of their rebellion against God, they would suffer the consequences of their disobedience, but God was always faithful to them.

Eventually God the Father sent Jesus the Son to earth to establish a new covenant, a new promise to His creation. Since the world began, when God makes a promise, He keeps it. We have the Holy Spirit as the guarantee that God will keep His promise of a grand inheritance for those who have heard the gospel and believed in Christ. Paul tells the Ephesians of the coming inheritance. He then spends the rest of the letter telling the Christians in Ephesus how to live a life in response to this promised inheritance in Christ. Faith, love, unity, imitating Christ, donning the "whole armor of God," and much more are part of Paul's instructions to the Christians in Ephesus. May we, with personal humility but with confidence in the Father, the Son, and the Spirit, lay claim to these blessings in Christ and the inheritance to come.

WRAPPING IT UP

Other writers of this book will discuss the many blessings we have in Christ and Paul's prayer for the readers of his letter to the church in Ephesus, but I wanted to comment on a concern related to failure to have an appreciation of the things discussed in this first chapter of Ephesians. My concern is the impact of anxiety and depression, particularly among Christian women. I think an inability to enjoy the peace that comes from a right relationship with God and His Son, and from the sense that the Holy Spirit is working in the lives of Christians, negatively impacts many Christians. In 1984, Billie Silvey wrote:

> In an increasingly impersonal world, it's easy to lose a sense of our own worth. Low self-esteem has been identified as the number one problem plaguing women today. The breakdown of the family, increased mobility, the accelerating pace of life—all serve to isolate us from each other. We can conduct much of our business by inserting a card in a machine and punching in a secret code, never seeing another human face.[6]

How much more true these words are today than when they were penned almost forty years ago. The National Center for Health Statistics (NCHS) partnered with the Census Bureau to develop and administer the Household Pulse Survey to measure the well-being of the U.S. population during the COVID-19 pandemic. They started collecting data in April of 2020. The portion of the survey related to mental health showed 36 percent of respondents reported anxiety and/or depression. Thirteen months later, in May of 2021, 30 percent of the respondents to the same survey reported anxiety and depression—an improvement but still very high.[7] Dr. Joe Rubino, CEO of the Center for Personal Reinvention, reports 85 percent of people worldwide have problems with self-esteem.[8] Even without the studies, just watching the evening news will show you that mental health and mental health services are a problem in our country and around the world. Isolation during the COVID-19 pandemic, increased online shopping, live-stream church, social media relationships, and many other changes have all altered how we relate to and interact with other people and even how we engage in worship.

God desires a relationship with His creation to the extent that He sent His Son to dwell among us, and He allowed His creation to crucify His Son (John 3:16). We matter to God, and we have value to Him. He has provided for us many blessings in Christ and has given us the Holy Spirit to give us confidence in His plan to bless us both now and in the future. Let's soak that in and let it help us to be at peace with ourselves and enjoy these lavish gifts from God.

PRAYER

God, thank You for blessing me with Your Spirit, the seal of Your guaranteed promise in my life. Help me to let your Spirit guide me in all that I do as I live in response to this precious gift.

QUESTIONS

1. How does the Holy Spirit mark you as God's?
2. How was the Spirit involved in the fulfillment of God's promises in the Old Testament?

3. What is the significance of something being "sealed" with a "pledge"? What does that say about the way God views His people?

4. How does the presence of the Holy Spirit in your life affect your relationship with God?

Chapter 10

The Hope of His Calling

Ephesians 1:18

Lori Boyd

ONE MAIN THING

The apostle Paul valued prayer. His writings reveal a man who believed in its power and who encouraged its practice. On occasion, he included the words of a prayer within the text of his letters so that his readers might know the petitions he begged of God on their behalf. In the Ephesians epistle, after a brief greeting and an outpouring of praise for the spiritual blessings found in Christ, Paul recounted his prayer for the saints in Ephesus, being aware of their continued faith in Jesus and love for fellow Christians. This prayer, found in Ephesians 1:15–23, began with Paul's thankfulness for his brothers and sisters in Ephesus and then centered on his request for God to grant them a "spirit of wisdom and of revelation in the knowledge of him" (Eph 1:17 ESV). The Ephesians had been enlightened when they heard and obeyed the gospel, and Paul prayed that they would grow in that illumination.[1] Paul desired for them to gain a deeper understanding in three specific areas: the hope of God's calling, the riches of God's inheritance, and the greatness of God's power. From the pages of the Bible, Paul's prayer is perpetually lifted up to God on behalf of Christians today for the same reason: to know God's purpose and to recognize our position relative to Him because of Christ. Paul's first appeal, in Ephesians 1:18, is "that you may know what is the hope to which he has called you." This inspires two questions: "How has God called you?" And, "What is the hope?"

INTRODUCTION

To understand "the hope" that Paul mentioned in Ephesians 1:18, it is necessary to first define the call, as the latter is foundational to the former. The call of God is described previously in verses 3–14. It is His divine invitation that is extended to all people for the gift of salvation that comes through Jesus Christ. In verse 4, we read that God chose us "in him" before the foundation of the world; and in verse 5, that "through Jesus Christ" He predestined us for adoption as His children. In verses 6 through 10, we read that we have redemption and forgiveness because of the riches of God's grace that came in the form of his Son, in whom all things would be united in heaven and on earth according to God's eternal purpose. In verse 11, we read that we have obtained an inheritance "in him"; and in verse 12, we find that we have hope "in Christ." Paul explained to the Christians in Ephesus that they had been placed in line for all of those blessings because of their response to the word of truth, when they believed in Christ, the gospel of their salvation. This is the specific manner in which we receive God's calling: through the word of truth, the gospel of Jesus Christ, our salvation.[2] When Paul wrote his second letter to the Thessalonians, he explained that they had been called by God "through our gospel" (2 Thess 2:14). He described the gospel to the Corinthians as the death, burial, and resurrection of Jesus and reminded them that he had preached the gospel to them, they had received it, they were standing in it, and (as long as they held tightly to the word he had preached to them) they were being saved by it (1 Cor 15:1–4). Those who respond to the gospel by obedience are referred to as "the called" (Rom 1:6).

God's call invites us into a relationship with Him through the reconciliatory work of Jesus. It is a call to eternal salvation that can be either accepted or rejected. It is a call that is for everyone, although not everyone will answer it (Matt 22:14). Some will hear the message of truth and choose to not believe. Others will hear it, believe it, and allow their lives to be transformed by it. Later, in Ephesians 4, Paul urged his readers to "walk in a manner worthy of the calling" to which they had been called (Eph 4:1). Even now, his inspired words continue to give exhortation to Christians: that our daily lives reflect who we have become in Christ by faithfully responding to God's call to salvation through His Son.

GOING DEEPER

Hope is the end result of God's call. God has offered salvation through Jesus, and those who believe and receive His gracious gift through obedience have hope. What is that hope? Often, in the English language, we use the word "hope" to describe something that we *want* to happen or *want* to be true, but not necessarily with any degree of confidence. We might use "hope" in the same way we would use the word "wish." It carries with it an aspect of uncertainty. That is not the hope we read about in the Bible as it relates to our position in Christ and the blessings that come from that relationship. According to the Greek-English Lexicon of the New Testament (BDAG), the Greek word for "hope" is *elpis*, and it means "the looking forward to something with some reason for confidence regarding fulfillment" and can also be translated "expectation."[3] God's call is an invitation to salvation found in His Son that is received through the message of the gospel and that results in hope—a hope that is anticipated with confidence.

In the context of Ephesians chapter one, the hope of God's calling that Paul prays the Ephesian Christians will come to know is the sum of all of the spiritual blessings that are found in Christ: adoption as God's children, redemption through His blood, forgiveness of sins, unity in Him in heaven and on earth, and the obtaining of an eternal inheritance. Paul's letter aimed to repair the division between the Jews and Gentiles that continued to trouble the early church. His message centered on the oneness that is achieved in Christ. Gentiles, who were at one time separated from Christ, having no hope, and without God, had been "brought near by the blood of Christ" (Eph 2:12–13). Jews and Gentiles were unified in Christ, reconciled to God, and fellow citizens of the household of God, which is the church (Eph 2:14–22). God's call was not only for the Jews—it was for all people, for all time; and through obedience to the call that was delivered to them in the message of the gospel, Gentiles could also share in the unsearchable riches of Christ. They now had hope. Even today, when the gospel is preached, God is calling people to the hope that can be found only in His Son.

The hope of the Christian has everything to do with Jesus:

- Because of Jesus, we have the hope of the gospel (Col 1:23).
- Because of Jesus, we have hope in eternal life (Titus 1:2).
- Because of Jesus, we have hope in salvation (1 Thess 5:8).
- Because of Jesus, we have hope of righteousness (Gal 5:5).
- Because of Jesus, we have hope laid up for us in heaven (Col 1:5).

Hope is founded on what Jesus has done, what He is doing now, and what He is going to do. He conquered sin, He was victorious over death, He advocates on our behalf in the presence of God, and He is coming back one day to take the members of His body to a place He has prepared for us (John 14:1–4). As Christians, our hope is the indescribable gift of Jesus Christ and the manifold blessings that are promised to those who are in Him. This hope is not "wishful thinking"! The hope we have in Jesus is a "sure and steadfast anchor of the soul" (Heb 6:19). It is strong enough to endure every storm, for every person, for all of time. It is immovable and trustworthy. It is the reason for God's call—He is inviting us to a place of hope.

WRAPPING IT UP

God's call rang out before the foundation of the world. He has called all people to eternal life that is available only in His Son, and His call is received in the form of the gospel message—the life, death, and resurrection of Jesus Christ. Anyone can accept the call of the gospel, which happens through hearing the word of God and responding in faithful obedience, but many will choose to reject it. The hope of God's calling is the expectation of the spiritual blessings that come to those who are in Christ. These spiritual blessings include adoption as children of God, redemption, forgiveness, unity in heaven and on earth, and an eternal inheritance. As Christians, we hope for our salvation—we are *certain* of it—not only in the present sense of salvation from sin, but also in the future sense that will be realized when Jesus comes again.

What does "the hope of God's calling" look like in our lives today? First, it looks like relationships. Positioning ourselves in Christ means that we are a part of His body, the church. In Christ's body, there is connection with Him as well as connection with other members. There is unity. There is edification. There is service. There is peace. There is love. But these things do not just happen. We must intentionally pursue them through the development of relationships.

Next, "the hope of God's calling" looks like joy: a gladness of the heart. We live for something better than this world, something that we happily anticipate, and it is all wrapped up in the hope that has been promised to those who are in Christ. *The New Bible Dictionary* defines joy as

> a quality, and not simply an emotion, grounded upon God himself and indeed derived from him, which characterizes the Christian's life on earth, and also anticipates eschatologically the joy of being with Christ forever in the kingdom of heaven.[4]

We choose joy because God chose us in Christ, and, because of that, we have hope. Joy remains in times of trial, in times of sadness, and in times of uncertainty because our joy is based on the unchanging truth that we have salvation in Jesus Christ.

Finally, "the hope of God's calling" in our lives today looks like endurance. We persevere in this life, because we *know* we have eternal life to come (1 John 5:12). The only way to lose our hope is to give up on our faith and separate ourselves from the body of Christ. Therefore, we stay strong, keep pressing forward, and do not quit, because we have been called by God to the hope—the confident expectation—of eternal life in His Son (1 John 5:11).

Between the covers of our Bibles, we read the story of God's love for mankind and our redemption through His Son, Jesus Christ—a story that we might appropriately entitle "The Hope of His Calling."

PRAYER

God of hope, thank You for calling me into the "expectation of what is certain," this new life through relationship with You. Help me to live worthy of that calling as I live in community with Your church and spread the joy of that hope to others.

QUESTIONS

1. Have you been answering the call of the Lord or of the world this week?
2. What hope do you find in answering God's call?
3. Hope is referred to in Scripture as a door (Hos 2:15), an anchor (Heb 6:19), and a helmet (1 Thess 5:8). Which of those images speaks most to you and why?

4. How do we decide whether something we hope to receive from God is a guarantee from Him, or a wish of ours? What would be an example for each category?

Chapter 11

Praise to His Glory

Ephesians 1:6, 12, 14

Stacy Harmon

ONE MAIN THING

When my two daughters were small children, their rooms were always a mess. I would tell them every few days to go clean their rooms. They would ask to work together, but they would inevitably get distracted and start to play. When I started down the hall to check on them, I would hear a flurry of activity, and one of them would shriek, "Oh, no! Here comes Momma!" When I opened the door, it was obvious they had just jumped up and started to work. My husband and I were constantly having to remind them, "Do your work first! Don't play until your work is done!" When they were bickering, I would say, "Be kind to your sister!" I did not tell them only once that they should look both ways before crossing the street and consider the matter settled; I told them every time we crossed a street. Why do parents repeat important instructions to the point of total exasperation?

We want our children to be good and safe and to grow up to be Christian adults.

God, our spiritual Father, also uses repetition to emphasize important instructions that will teach His children to behave in a manner that is pleasing to Him. Because "praise of His glory" (or a variation thereof) is mentioned three separate times in Ephesians 1 (verses 6, 12, 14), we can determine that it is a phrase deserving of our serious consideration. Paul wants his readers to get the message: A vital function of a Christian is to demonstrate praise for God's glory. Because Ephesians 1 instructs God's children to offer "praise of His glory," we must fully comprehend what this phrase means, why we should praise His glory, and how we accomplish it.

GOING DEEPER

Praise is a behavior we already understand and appreciate in our relationships with others. We are sometimes uncomfortable or embarrassed when another offers us praise, but we usually appreciate being recognized for our efforts. The best supervisors offer compliments when their employees deserve them. Teachers use behavior charts and positive reinforcement to encourage the conduct they desire from their students. Parents offer candy and proud exclamations of praise when toilet training their toddlers. Sunday school teachers make attendance charts so children will tell their parents they want to come to class. We give children prizes for coming to Vacation Bible School or bringing a friend. Nearly everyone responds positively to praise because we understand that it frequently expresses approval, acceptance, or love.

As a teacher, I have loved all of my students, but sometimes one comes along who is difficult for me to handle. I had one such student in a high school class a few years ago. He seemed to possess a special insight into every possible method to annoy me, and he used each method daily! He was flippant, disinterested, and disrespectful. After months of having this young man test my patience, I realized that my sanity would require that I approach him with a different tactic. After taking it to God in prayer several times, I felt compelled to try praise. I began to look more carefully for the positive aspects of his behavior and praise him both publicly and privately. Soon, his behavior improved enough that I no longer felt that each day was a test of my patience and an exercise in restraining my tongue. He, like most of us, responded positively to praise.

God also desires our praise, but the praise we should offer to Him is on a completely different level than that we offer to each other. Our praise to God must be more than merely expressing appreciation for a favor, offering a compliment for accomplishing a small task, or telling Him we appreciate a behavior of which we approve. Instead, we should offer continual expressions of adoration and appreciation to our Father in honor of His goodness and power.

Nowhere in the Bible is praise more completely demonstrated than in the book of Psalms. There are 182 instances of the word "praise" in the Psalms (NIV), including the singing of praise (Ps 7:17), declaring His praises (Ps 9:14), and proclaiming His praise (Ps 26:7). Remember that the more a command or example is repeated, the more important it is to follow. If the psalmists of whom God approves repeat their praise of Him nearly 200 times, then we should certainly be offering our own praise as often as we can!

Our lives must emulate this attitude of praise. We should be glorifying God in whatever we do, wherever we go, and to whomever we meet. Our prayers, our worship, our conduct, and our very lives are to extol the greatness of God. We sometimes think our worship is what happens on Sunday, but an adopted child of God must be praising Him every day. Our daily praise should be purposeful and intentional. We should also exhibit a quiet type of praise that others recognize in the way we live our lives and conduct ourselves in our relationships, a sort of praise that shows we are children of God and glorifies Him.

If one hundred people were asked what first comes to mind when they hear the word "glory," they would probably provide nearly one hundred different answers. Some people might immediately associate "glory" with a biblical concept. Others might imagine a scene from the 1989 movie *Glory* with Denzel Washington as a Civil War soldier. Perhaps a song like "The Battle Hymn of the Republic" comes to mind. Some might envision Old

Glory waving in the breeze. Morning glory flowers in their fleeting beauty might be the answer for some. Whatever the word "glory" evokes in our minds, we understand that glory has to do with admiration, respect, or praise.

We all have some basic understanding of the word "glory," but basic is all it is. We understand simple, earthly glory, but God's glory is greater than we can fathom. This world, with all its sin and flawed people, has no form of glory that comes close to comparing to the glory of God. God sent His Son, Jesus, to this earth to live amongst man. This world had never seen, nor will ever see, another like Jesus; Jesus is the perfect and sinless Savior of all mankind. Even while living as a man, Jesus reflected the glory of the Father. John tells us that "the Word became flesh and made his dwelling among us. We have seen his glory, the glory of the one and only Son, who came from the Father, full of grace and truth" (John 1:14).

In Ephesians 1:4–14, Paul offers numerous reasons why Christians should praise God's glory. Paul's first mention of "praise of his glorious grace" (Eph 1:6) is preceded by his description of us as blessed with spiritual blessings (verse 3), chosen to be holy and blameless (verse 4), and adopted to sonship (verse 5). God's blessing us and making us His children should fill us with such gratitude that we can't help but praise Him. Because of the hope we have in Christ, we praise His glory (verse 12). Through Christ and the Holy Spirit, our inheritance is guaranteed (verse 14). We have countless reasons to be thankful to God and to express our thankfulness for His goodness, grace, love, and adoption of us. As His children, we recognize and stand in awe of His glory.

WRAPPING IT UP

As a child, I first discovered morning glory flowers in my grandmother's backyard one beautiful summer morning. I excitedly called Grandma over to show her my lovely discovery. My ever-practical Grandma declared them to be weeds and explained that they would close up later in the day and no longer be beautiful. I was so disappointed to learn that the flowers' beauty had no endurance.

These flowers are the perfect example of the types of glory man often seeks; our earthly endeavors may appear to be beautiful for a moment, but they quickly fade. The glory of God, however, is not temporal or earthly; it is eternal and heavenly and truly worthy of praise. We should be focused on the kinds of lasting treasures God has offered us through His Son:

> Do not store up for yourselves treasures on earth, where moths and vermin destroy, and where thieves break in and steal. But store up for yourselves treasures in heaven, where moths and vermin do not destroy, and where thieves do not break in and steal. For where your treasure is, there your heart will be also. (Matt 6:19–21)

Praising His glory is one way we can be storing up treasures in heaven and focusing on truly important matters.

We serve as vessels of praise for God's glory, not only because Ephesians 1 tells us that we are, but also so that we can shine like stars among this warped and crooked generation (Phil 2:15). This world can be a place of beauty, but it can also be a place of heartache and sin. As the children of God, we are supposed to be different. We are to shine our lights and do good works so that others will join us in glorifying God (Matt 5:16). Offering praise to His glory allows us to reflect His goodness and bring a little light to this darkness in which we must exist for a time.

Our lives should serve as an example to others to demonstrate the blessings of being a Christian. Even though Christians share in the struggles of this world, we know that our Father is going to make it all better in eternity. Our reward for persevering is more valuable than anything we can find in this life, so we can keep praising God for His love and blessings. Our adoption as children of the Almighty enables us to endure the troubles of this world. We can one day be at home with our Father. He will welcome us and give us an eternal home unlike anything we can find in this life. If that is not a cause for praising His glory, I don't know what is!

PRAYER

Glorious God, I praise You with all that I am! You are wonderful; You are powerful; You are glorious. May I live my life in acknowledgment of You.

QUESTIONS

1. What is glory? What is God's glory?
2. How are you showing God's glory to others in your everyday interactions?
3. What aspects of God's nature should we praise? Give Scriptures to support your answers.
4. When is it NOT appropriate to praise God?

Chapter 12

This Is the Power of Christ in Me

Ephesians 1:19–21

Jeanne Foust

ONE MAIN THING

So far, so good. Every spiritual blessing we've studied—our adoption as His children, our holy and blameless status, the grace and favor we receive, redemption, forgiveness, knowledge of His will, an eternal inheritance, the Holy Spirit, hope, the church as our spiritual family—is found not only in Christ but also in Christ *alone*. There is nowhere else to benefit from these blessings, no other source for all this goodness.

But what does that mean for the way we go about leading this life on earth? Blessings too awesome to comprehend fully empower us, again through Christ, to live lives of faith, grace, courage, joy, and boldness not because of us, but because of His power in us. To be truthful, a life transformed by the power of Christ looks strange in this world: It isn't self-seeking (1 Cor 13:5

NIV), doesn't worry about the "stuff" of life in the same way (Matt 6:25–34), and is filled with joy, not because our circumstances are always ideal (Jas 1:2), but because our minds can be set on things above (Col 3:1) and our sights on eternity (Eccl 3:11). The challenge, then, is stepping fully and confidently into our role as "the-power-of-Christ-in-me" kind of Christians and living boldly for Him.

GOING DEEPER

Near the very end of Ephesians 1, Paul prays that the "eyes of your heart may be enlightened" to the hope to which Christians have been called and also to a "glorious inheritance" (Eph 1:18). It's safe to say most of us are on board with those promises: We can live lives of hope because we're anticipating a glorious inheritance. Yes, sign me up! Paul's prayer probably rises out of his knowledge that we, as humans living in a fallen world, might be prone to lose sight of this great truth and incredible promise.

If the laundry list of promises in Christ had ended there, not one of us would have felt shortchanged; we do not deserve all these blessings in Christ laid out throughout Scripture and specifically here in Ephesians 1. But He's not done. In verse 19 Paul adds "and his incomparably great power for us who believe." This part of the promise feels somewhat less accessible, maybe even more mysterious. How does that "power of Christ in me" work?

We acknowledge He has tremendous power; we've seen it and believe it through Scripture. His power is unsurpassed and unparalleled. But how do we tap into that "incomparably great power"? He *says* it is "for us who believe"! It's ours for the claiming, so why don't we understand it and embrace it?

If there's any doubt about what this power is exactly (I suspect Paul knew we would be incredulous), he adds this clarification in verses 19–20: "That power is the same as the mighty strength he exerted when he raised Christ from the dead and seated him at his right hand in the heavenly realms." This power is the same power we saw in the resurrection of Jesus? We have access to "resurrection power" in Christ![1] We know one day the dead in Christ will rise (1 Thess 4:16), but this verse indicates the power of Christ is living and equipping us to live for Him in the present. It's the difference in death vs. life—hope in our adversity, forgiveness in our sin, rich life in our spiritual poverty. Life is not futile because we have the power of Christ in us. In fact, the opposite is true: Life is purposeful and beautiful even in its imperfection because the power of Christ lives in us.

Furthermore, Paul appropriately reiterates Christ's superiority over humankind, thereby acknowledging the authority and preeminence of His power in our lives. When Paul writes "far above all rule and authority, power and dominion, and every name that is invoked" (Eph 1:21), he is saying no ruler, power, government, entity, or force overshadows the authority and power inherent in

Christ. That power teaches us not only to "render to Caesar the things that are Caesar's" (Matt 22:21 ESV) but also to have the confidence to speak up and stand up for God's principles in our often-godless world. We can step into our calling to be the hands and feet of Jesus with the assurance that we have His blessing and His power on our side. When we embrace this power of Christ, we have both humility *and* boldness, and our words and actions bring glory and attention to *Him*, not to *us*.

Paul finally and helpfully provides a time reference in verse 21. He is obviously speaking to the Ephesian church but not to them only; he's writing to us as well. God's sovereign power was real in biblical times and still is in our day, "not only in the present age but also in the one to come" (Eph 1:21 NIV). Our day is not too godless for Christ's power to speak life into it. Our lives are not too futile for Christ's power to bring them purpose and beauty. Our despair is not too great for Him, our disappointment is not too much for Him, our faith is not too lacking for Him. The power of Christ that makes dead things alive is at work in us, in our churches, and in our world through us!

So the implications are both personal and far-reaching. This power of Christ is available and working in each of us as individual Christians, but Paul is writing to the *church* in Ephesus. Imagine the potential when we gather as Christians in churches and tap into the power of Christ at work in us collectively. The collective church has the potential to change the world by reaching the lost and providing hope to the underserved, and that potential is made possible by the power of Christ at work within Christians and the Christian church around the globe. What an awesome purpose to be a small part of changing the world because of Him, through Him, and for Him!

When Paul writes in Philippians 4:13, "I can do all things through Christ who strengthens me" (NKJV), we see this same principle at work. In fact, this theme of Christ's power and its availability to us is at the heart of Paul's many letters. Had he italicized the important words in the often-quoted Philippians verse, would he have italicized "I" or "through Christ"? It is through Christ—in Him—that we accomplish anything—not because of our credentials—and He strengthens us with His "incomparably great power." In our human-centric and self-centered thinking we sometimes assign the ability to accomplish (in this context, to endure or transcend) "all things" to ourselves and award Jesus a supporting role; the reverse is actually true, and we would be wise to rethink those roles.

Perhaps the best way to understand the transformative power of Christ in the Christian life is to see it in context: How does someone who fully embraces the power of Christ live life? What does it look like for a God-follower to claim the power of Christ in his or her life, and how does it transform that life into one that is almost not recognizable or sensible in this world? One of the best examples of this "power-of-Christ-in-me" life is Elisabeth Elliot. Here's her amazing story in the shortest version possible, but the whole story is well worth the investment of time.

Elisabeth and her husband Jim were missionaries to the Quichua Indian tribe in the Amazonian jungle of Ecuador in the 1950s. Her husband and four other missionaries had been making their way into the remote and dangerous Auca tribe—had been trying to build relationships and trust through humanitarian efforts—and were starting to make contact when all five men were speared to death in early 1956. Elizabeth, along with her ten-month-old daughter, continued to work with the Quichua tribe and was eventually invited to live among and minister to the very tribe who murdered her husband Jim and four others. Teaching forgiveness and grace through her example, she ended up leading the Auca people to Jesus despite tremendous personal loss and grief.[2] Years later Elisabeth wrote, "The secret of joy is Christ in me, not me in a different set of circumstances."[3] She found joy not because her circumstances were perfect (far from it!) but because He —and His power—were at home in her, and the peace, purpose, and joy that knowledge brought trumped any ideal circumstances. *This* was the power of Christ in her, and it *still* makes no human sense! It is, in fact, supernatural. Grace upon grace!

WRAPPING IT UP

Our personal stories may not be as dramatic or inspirational as Elisabeth Elliot's. Ours may not be ones of martyrdom and grace and redemption, but the truth remains: The same power that spoke this earth into existence, assured victory to His people when they faced seemingly insurmountable odds, used messed up and broken people to accomplish His holy purposes, and raised Jesus from the dead—it lives in us. He *chooses* for His power to live in us. *This* is the power of Christ in me, that I believe in His power to change me and to change the world, and it equips us all to serve selflessly, live boldly, and speak unashamedly. It blesses us and others in this life and for all eternity in our glorious inheritance. However imperfect, life can be rich and good and deep and purposeful and beautiful when we embrace these overwhelmingly wonderful blessings. Now, let's go claim the good life available in Christ and Christ alone!

PRAYER

Almighty God, how often I let my own weakness limit Your resurrection power in me! Use Your power to help me to be mighty as I strive to live in the fullness of Christ, with His love, wisdom, grace, and sacrifice. May I never rely on my own strength, but always rest in Yours.

QUESTIONS

1. What keeps the power of Christ from reaching its maximum potency in you?
2. What is our role in utilizing the power of Christ?

3. How is the power of Christ still active in you when you're facing situations or problems you cannot change?
4. Who can you tell about the blessings in Christ found in Ephesians 1 and studied in this book?

Appendix A — Scripture Writing/Reading Plan

Scripture copying is beneficial for many reasons. It helps to focus our thoughts and allows us to meditate on God's word. If you learn visually or kinetically, it is an excellent way to engrain the word more deeply in your mind. Often when copying Scripture, patterns and repeated words become more evident than when simply reading the words on the page.

Below is a suggested schedule to follow if you would like to copy the book of Ephesians during the time you are reading this book. It has been suggested that there are as many as 54 blessings of being in Christ found in chapters 1–3 alone![1] Try to identify them as you copy. You can copy all the verses for each week in one sitting or divide it up throughout the week by writing a couple of verses a day.

Week 1 1:1–14

Week 2 1:15–23

Week 3 2:1–10

Week 4 2:11–22

Week 5 3:1–13

Week 6 3:14–21

Week 7 4:1–16

Week 8 4:17–5:5

Week 9 5:6–21

Week 10 5:22–33

Week 11 6:1–9

Week 12 6:10–20

Week 13 6:21–24

Appendix B — Prayers

Ch 1 Every Spiritual Blessing

God, thank You for blessing me. I know I have done nothing to deserve Your bountiful gifts. Help me to place more value on the spiritual blessings I have received than the physical things I can see with my eyes. Thank you for Jesus, who made it possible for me to partake in such wonderful eternal blessings.

Ch 2 Adoption

Abba Father, thank You for making the decision to call me Your own. Thank You for showing me care and compassion as your child every day. Help me never to forget that I am Yours.

Ch 3 Sanctification

Holy God, sanctify me. Help my heart and my mind to think on You always. You have lifted me out of darkness, and I long to walk in Your holiness for the rest of my days. Cleanse me from all of my impurities.

Ch 4 Grace and Favor

Gracious Lord, thank You for leaning toward me and being attentive to my life and who I am. Help me to live a life in gratitude for Your grace. Lord, I deserve nothing You have offered, yet You give freely anyway. Help me to rest in Your leaning and extend that grace to those around me.

Ch 5 Redemption

Precious Savior, thank You for being willing to redeem me from all my faults. Help me to remember I could not be saved without Your redeeming blood, and help me to stay grateful and humble in this all of my days.

Ch 6 Forgiveness

Dear Lord, thank You for the ability to see who You are, to see through You what I lack, and to come to You to be made whole. Help me to lay aside my pride so that I may be reconciled to and in relationship with You. Your forgiveness is greater than my sin, and I will forever be grateful.

Ch 7 Knowledge

God of truth, help me never to stop in my pursuit of knowledge inspired by You. Help me to stay hungry for Your word and joyful in the pursuit. Give me the strength to lay aside my pride, so I can fully receive the wisdom You offer from above.

Ch 8 Inheritance

O God, my portion, thank You for bringing me into Your family so that I may take part in Your immeasurable inheritance. Help me to understand that, as Your adopted heir, I should act in ways befitting one who is called Your daughter.

Ch 9 Holy Spirit

God, thank You for blessing me with Your Spirit, the seal of Your guaranteed promise in my life. Help me to let your Spirit guide me in all that I do as I live in response to this precious gift.

Ch 10 The Hope of His Calling

God of hope, thank You for calling me into the "expectation of what is certain," this new life through relationship with You. Help me to live worthy of that calling as I live in community with Your church and spread the joy of that hope to others.

Ch 11 Praise to His Glory

Glorious God, I praise You with all that I am! You are wonderful; You are powerful; You are glorious. May I live my life in acknowledgment of You.

Ch 12 This Is the Power of Christ in Me!

Almighty God, how often I let my own weakness limit Your resurrection power in me! Use Your power to help me to be mighty as I strive to live in the fullness of Christ, with His love, wisdom, grace, and sacrifice. May I never rely on my own strength, but always rest in Yours.

Appendix C — Reflection Questions

Ch 1 Every Spiritual Blessing

1. How does thinking of the definition of the Greek word *eulogia* challenge the Western concept of being blessed?
2. If you are in Christ, the blessings of Ephesians 1 are already yours. Which blessings do you need to more fully recognize and thank God for?
3. We often have a tendency to refer to blessings as the physical things in life. Why can this be problematic? What intentional actions can you take to be more aware of your spiritual blessings?
4. If all your physical blessings were taken away tomorrow, would you be content with your spiritual blessings alone?

Ch 2 Adoption

1. What baggage do you bring to your relationship with God?
2. How does it make you feel knowing that God is committed to us like a parent, no matter how broken or distant we might be?
3. Our adoption in Christ offers us continual connection to our Father. How does He continually reach out to us? What is our avenue for responding?
4. In what ways do you see God's deliberate love for you, His adopted child? How do your actions reflect gratitude for that love?

Ch 3 Sanctification

1. Describe how sanctification is both a state of being for the Christian and also a never-ending process. In other words, how are you both *sanctified* and *being sanctified*?
2. What is keeping your heart and mind from being fully pure? What are you clinging to that is hindering your thoughts from remaining on Him and on righteousness?
3. Thinking about your sanctification through prayer, the word, fellowship, and gratefulness—which of these comes most naturally to you? Which do you need to be more intentional about making a part of your spiritual life?

4. What are some practical ways you choose to be "set apart" from the world? Are there certain activities you choose not to engage in? Places you won't go? What does the tension of "in the world but not of the world" look like in your life?

Ch 4 Grace and Favor

1. How do you see God's attentiveness and care in your daily life?
2. What things in your life make it difficult to lean back toward God as He leans into you?
3. What are you doing in response to the grace and favor you receive from God?
4. When you think of grace as a space to live rather than an object to grasp, how does that affect your previous ideas and beliefs about grace?
5. What other spaces do we often find ourselves living in rather than grace (examples: perfectionism, comparison, etc.)?

Ch 5 Redemption

1. Redemption can mean being saved from evil or restoring what was lost. Which of these do you think requires the most grace from God—saving us from our sins or restoring to us the blessings He promised? Why?
2. Have you ever been rescued from disaster (literally or figuratively)? What was it like? How

can you rescue others and point them to God at the same time?

3. How would you explain the full, biblical concept of redemption to someone who doesn't know much about the Bible?
4. What can you change in your life right now to demonstrate that you have been redeemed?

Ch 6 Forgiveness

1. How does Paul's backstory make his teaching on forgiveness so powerful?
2. Can you identify the time in your life when you recognized Jesus, repented, and were reconciled to God?
3. Where are you currently falling short of the perfection of Jesus? For what sins do you currently need the blessing of forgiveness?
4. How does forgiveness unburden us? Can you think of a personal relationship that was unburdened by forgiveness?

Ch 7 Knowledge

1. How does looking at knowledge as a blessing from God dispel pride?
2. How have you leaned on your own understanding in the past? How did that affect your faith?
3. What are some of the ways you have pursued godly knowledge today? This week? This year? Is that a priority in Your life?

4. Second Peter 1:5 urges us to add virtue to our faith and knowledge to our virtue. Why are faith and virtue listed as precursors to knowledge?

Ch 8 Inheritance

1. In what way is our inheritance something we experience in the present as well as the future?
2. Where is the Father trying to guide you, and what is stopping you from following Him?
3. The song "Mansion over the Hilltop" talks about wanting a luxurious mansion in heaven. Is that greedy? What should our attitude be toward our heavenly reward?
4. Besides salvation, what is the most valuable thing God has already given you?

Ch 9 Holy Spirit

1. How does the Holy Spirit mark you as God's?
2. How was the Spirit involved in the fulfillment of God's promises in the Old Testament?
3. What is the significance of something being "sealed" with a "pledge"? What does that say about the way God views His people?
4. How does the presence of the Holy Spirit in your life affect your relationship with God?

Ch 10 The Hope of His Calling

1. Have you been answering the call of the Lord or of the world this week?
2. What hope do you find in answering God's call?
3. Hope is referred to in Scripture as a door (Hos 2:15), an anchor (Heb 6:19), and a helmet (1 Thess 5:8). Which of those images speaks most to you and why?
4. How do we decide whether something we hope to receive from God is a guarantee from Him, or a wish of ours? What would be an example for each category?

Ch 11 Praise to His Glory

1. What is glory? What is God's glory?
2. How are you showing God's glory to others in your everyday interactions?
3. What aspects of God's nature should we praise? Give Scriptures to support your answers.
4. When is it NOT appropriate to praise God?

Ch 12 This Is the Power of Christ in Me!

1. What keeps the power of Christ from reaching its maximum potency in you?
2. What is our role in utilizing the power of Christ?
3. How is the power of Christ still active in you when you're facing situations or problems you cannot change?

4. Who can you tell about the blessings in Christ found in Ephesians 1 and studied in this book?

Appendix D — Bible Marking

Bible marking is a tool that can make Scripture more accessible and easy to reference. Below, you will find a series of Bible verses related to the topic studied in each chapter. This is not a comprehensive list of references; it is meant to provide an overview or snapshot of each concept that you can mark and study with others or on your own.

How to mark the Scriptures in your Bible is up to you. Some prefer to highlight the verses with a different color for each topic. Others use the blank pages in the front or back of a Bible to indicate the first verse in the "chain" so they can study the topic systematically. If using this method, you would then write the reference for the next verse in the margin beside the text of the first verse, and so on through the sequence. Write "stop" or draw a stop sign after the final verse. You may prefer simply to keep these studies in a notebook where you can add your own notes. There is no right or wrong way, so choose whatever works best for you.

Ch 1 Every Spiritual Blessing

Ephesians 1:3

Deuteronomy 7:12-15

Psalm 24:3-6

Psalm 133:1-3

Matthew 5:3-12

James 1:25

Revelation 22:14

Ch 2 Adoption

Ephesians 1:4-6

Deuteronomy 14:1-2

Isaiah 43:1

Hosea 11:1

Romans 8:15

2 Corinthians 6:16-18

Galatians 3:25-26

Galatians 4:4-7

Ch 3 Sanctification

Ephesians 1:4

Leviticus 20:26

Joshua 3:5

John 17:17–19

1 Corinthians 6:11

2 Corinthians 7:1

2 Timothy 2:21

1 Thessalonians 5:23

2 Thessalonians 2:13

Hebrews 2:11

Hebrews 10:9–14

Hebrews 13:12

Ch 4 Grace and Favor

Ephesians 1:5–8

Psalm 84:11

Romans 3:23–24

Romans 5:15–17

Romans 11:6

2 Corinthians 8:9

2 Corinthians 12:9

Ephesians 2:4-10

Ephesians 4:7

1 Timothy 1:14

Titus 2:11-13

I Peter 4:10

Ch 5 Redemption

Ephesians 1:7

Leviticus 25:23-28

Exodus 6:6-8

Job 19:25

Psalm 31:5

Psalm 34:22

Psalm 130:7-8

Isaiah 35

Isaiah 43:1-2

Romans 3:24-26

1 Corinthians 6:20

1 Corinthians 7:23

Galatians 3:13

Galatians 4:4–5

Colossians 1:14

Titus 2:14

Hebrews 9:12–15

1 Peter 1:18–19

Ch 6 Forgiveness

Ephesians 1:7

Psalm 32:5

Psalm 103:1–12

Isaiah 1:18

Isaiah 43:25

Matthew 6:14–15

Matthew 18:21–22

Acts 2:37–39

Acts 5:30–31

Acts 13:37–39

Ephesians 4:32

Colossians 3:13

1 John 1:7–9

Ch 7 Knowledge

Ephesians 1:9, 17

Proverbs 2:1–10

Proverbs 3:13

Proverbs 15:14

Proverbs 23:23

Hosea 6:3, 6

Amos 8:11–12

John 8:32, 55

Romans 11:33

Colossians 1:9

Colossians 2:2

Colossians 3:9–10

James 3:17

2 Peter 1:3–7

Ch 8 Inheritance

Ephesians 1:11, 14, 18

Psalm 61:5

Psalm 119:111

Acts 26:18

Colossians 1:12

Colossians 3:23–24

Titus 3:6–7

1 Peter 1:3–4

Ch 9 Holy Spirit

Ephesians 1:13–14

Genesis 1:2

Psalm 51:11

Psalm 143:10

Ezekiel 36:26–27

John 14:15–17

John 16:12–15

Acts 2:38

Romans 8:9, 26–27

Romans 15:13

1 Corinthians 2:10

I Corinthians 3:16–17

1 Corinthians 6:19–20

1 Corinthians 12:13

Galatians 5:22–23

Titus 3:5–6

Ch 10 The Hope of His Calling

Ephesians 1:18

Psalm 39:7

Hosea 2:15

Acts 24:15

Romans 4:18–21

Romans 5:3–5

Romans 8:24–25

Romans 15:4

Ephesians 4:1–6

Colossians 1:3–6, 22–23

2 Timothy 1:9–12

2 Thessalonians 2:13–17

Titus 2:12–13

Hebrews 6:17–19

1 Peter 1:3–4

1 Peter 3:15

Ch 11 Praise to His Glory

Ephesians 1:6, 12, 14

Psalm 19:1

Psalm 29:1–2

Psalm 96

Psalm 148:13

Isaiah 42:10-13

Romans 1:21

Romans 15:5–7

1 Corinthians 10:31

Ch 12 This is the Power of Christ in Me!

Ephesians 1:19–21

Isaiah 40:29

2 Corinthians 12:9

Galatians 2:20

Ephesians 3:10–12, 16–21

Ephesians 6:10

Philippians 4:13

Colossians 1:27

Endnotes

Introduction

[1]Justin Jeppsen, "Redeeming the Meaning of Blessing," *Strategic Renewal*, http://www.strategicrenewal.-com/redeeming-meaning-blessing/.

[2] Jack Finegan, *Light from the Ancient Past: The Archeological Background of the Hebrew-Christian Religion* (Princeton: Princeton University Press, 1974), 2:348.

[3] *New International Version Archaeological Study Bible* (Grand Rapids: Zondervan, 2005), 1,965.

[4] James S. Jeffers, *The Greco-Roman World of the New Testament Era: Exploring the Background of Early Christianity* (Downers Grove, IL: InterVarsity Press, 1999), 266.

[5] Quoted in Finegan, *Light from the Ancient Past*, 2:346.

[6] David Noel Freedman, ed., *The Anchor Bible Dictionary* (New York: Doubleday, 1992), 2:543.

[7] *NIV Archaeological Study Bible*, 1,968; Finegan, *Light from the Ancient Past*, 2:347, 2:349; Jeffers, *Greco-Roman World*, 68.

[8] Jeffers, *Greco-Roman World*, 57.

[9] Jeffers, *Greco-Roman World*, 117, 159, 266.

[10] Geoffrey W. Bromiley, ed., *The International Standard Bible Encyclopedia* (Grand Rapids: Eerdmans, 1982) 2:116.

[11] Jeffers, *Greco-Roman World*, 269.

[12] John R. W. Stott, *What Christ Thinks of the Church* (Grand Rapids: Eerdmans, 1972), 24.

[13] *NIV Archaeological Study Bible*, 1,968.

[14] H. Leo Boles, *A Commentary on Acts of the Apostles* (Nashville: Gospel Advocate, 1962), 16; J. W. McGarvey, *New Commentary on Acts of Apostles* (Cincinnati: Standard, 1892), 2:xxix.

[15] Don DeWelt, *Acts Made Actual* (Joplin, MO: College, 1974), 256.

[16] Wayne Jackson, *The Acts of the Apostles from Jerusalem to Rome*, 2nd ed. (Stockton, CA: Christian Courier, 2005), 230.

[17] David L. Roper, *Acts 15-28,* Truth for Today Commentary (Searcy, AR: Resource, 2001), 182.

[18] Jason C. Kuo, "Prison Letters," *The Lexham Bible Dictionary* (Bellingham, WA: Lexham Press, 2016), n.p.

[19] Francis Foulkes, *Ephesians: An Introduction and Commentary*, Tyndale New Testament Commentaries 10 (Downers Grove, IL: InterVarsity Press, 1989), 25.

[20] Craig S. Keener, *The IVP Bible Background Commentary*, 2nd ed. (Downers Grove, IL: IVP Academic, 2014), 541–45.

Ch 1 Every Spiritual Blessing

[1] "εὐλογέω," *Blue Letter Bible* (2022), https://www.blueletterbible.org/lexicon/g2127/csb/mgnt/0-1/.

[2] Davon Huss, "A Little Boy Came to the Washington Monument," *Sermon Central* (2007), https://www.sermoncentral.com/sermon-illustrations/63821/on-stories-by-davon-huss.

[3] R. A. Torrey, "Daily Devotional Studies in the New Testament for Individual Meditation and Family Worship," *The King's Business* 9.6 (June 1918): 530.

[4] James Orr, ed., "Spiritual Blessing," *International Standard Bible Encyclopedia* (Grand Rapids: Eerdmans, 1939), https://www.internationalstandardbible.com/S/spiritual-blessing.html.

[5] F. F. Bruce, *The Gospel of John* (Grand Rapids: Eerdmans, 1983), 43.

Ch 3 Sanctification

[1] "Sanctification," *Merriam-Webster.com Dictionary* (2023), https://www.merriam-webster.com/dictionary/sanctification.

[2] "Sanctify," *Merriam-Webster.com Dictionary* (2023), https://www.merriam-webster.com/dictionary/sanctify.

[3] Cleveland Clinic, "You Are Your Brain" (2023), https://healthybrains.org/brain-facts/.

[4] James Burton Coffman, *Commentary on Philippians* (Abilene, TX: Abilene Christian University Press, 1983–1999), https://www.studylight.org/commentaries/eng/bcc/philippians-4.html.

[5] Coffman, *Commentary on Philippians*, https://www.studylight.org/commentaries/eng/bcc/philippians-4.html.

[6] Laura Jenkins, *Thought Garden* (Self-published, 2021), 10.

[7] Jenkins, *Thought Garden*, 11.

[8] David Lipscomb, *A Commentary on the New Testament Epistles: Ephesians, Philippians, and Colossians*, ed. J. W. Shepherd (Nashville: Gospel Advocate, 1989), 226.

[9] Paul David Tripp, *War of Words: Getting to the Heart of Your Communication Problems* (Phillipsburg, NJ: P&R Publishing, 2000), 55.

[10] Dietrich Bonhoeffer, *Life Together* (New York: Harper & Row, 1956), 91–92.

Ch 4 Grace and Favor

[1] "xáris," *HELPS Word Studies* (Discovery Bible: 2021), https://biblehub.com/greek/5485.htm.

[2] Dennis J. Hester, comp., *The Vance Havner Quote Book: Sparkling Gems from the Most Quoted Preacher in America* (Grand Rapids: Baker, 1986), 105.

Ch 5 Redemption

[1] Fanny Crosby, "Redeemed, How I Love to Proclaim It," (1882).

[2] William Cowper, "There Is a Fountain," (1771).

[3] "Redemption," *Oxford English Dictionary* (Oxford: Oxford University Press, 2012).

[4] Rick Hampson, "Raymond Dunn, 'Gerber Boy,' Dead at 20," *AP News* (26 January 1995), https://apnews.-com/article/14ff81b4287c4a21bce361563cc34a69.

[5] Billy Witz, "U.S. Soccer Player Is National Hero (in Honduras)," *New York Times* (22 January 2010), https://www.nytimes.com/2010/01/23/sports/soccer/23soccer.html.

Ch 7 Knowledge

[1] Cathy Turner, "Teach" *Courier Journal* (Florence, AL: 26 February 2020), 26. Article has been edited for inclusion in this chapter.

[2] Randy Gill, "The Magnificat," (2003).

Ch 8 Inheritance

[1] Elka Klein, "Splitting Heirs: Patterns of Inheritance among Barcelona's Jews," *Jewish History* 16:1 (2002): 49.

[2] Klein, "Splitting Heirs," 49; Martine Segalen, "Gender and Inheritance Patterns in Rural Europe: Women as Wives, Widows, Daughters and Sisters," *History and Anthropology* 32:2 (2021): 171–87.

[3] Segalen, "Gender and Inheritance Patterns," 171–87.

[4] Diana Burrell, "Here's the Difference Between an Heir and a Beneficiary," *MoneyWisdom* (23 Feb 2023), https://go.hfcu.org/blog/whats-the-difference-between-an-heir-and-a-beneficiary.

[5] "Can We Really Inherit Trauma?," *New York Times* (10 Dec 2018), https://www.nytimes.com/2018/12/10/health/mind-epigenetics-genes.html.

[6] Justin Taylor, "What Did the Temple Look Like in Jesus' Time?," *The Gospel Coalition* (13 July 2010), https://www.thegospelcoalition.org/blogs/justin-taylor/what-did-the-temple-look-like-in-jesus-time/.

[7] Jonathan H. Ohrt, Philip B. Clarke, and Abigail H. Conley, *Wellness Counseling: A Holistic Approach to Prevention and Intervention*, 4th ed. (Alexandria, VA: American Counseling Association, 2019), 146; David D. Chen, *Stress Management and Prevention: Applications to Daily Life*, 3rd ed. (New York: Routledge, 2017), 329.

Ch 9 Holy Spirit

[1] Leonard Allen, *Poured Out: The Spirit of God Empowering the Mission of God* (Abilene, TX: Abilene Christian University Press, 2018), 59–61.

[2] Paul D. Weaver, ed., *Surveying the Pauline Epistles* (Coppell, TX: Learn the Word Publishing, 2019), 130–131.

[3] James Strong, ed., "sphragizo," *The New Strong's Expanded Exhaustive Concordance of the Bible* (Nashville: Nelson, 2001), 244.

[4] James Strong, ed., "arrhabon," *The New Strong's Expanded Exhaustive Concordance of the Bible* (Nashville: Nelson, 2001), 42.

[5] Weaver, *Surveying the Pauline Epistles*, 131.

[6] Billie Silvey, *God Has a Plan for You: The Riches of Ephesians for Women* (Nashville: 20th Century Christian, 1984), 6.

[7] National Center for Health Statistics, "Anxiety and Depression: Household Pulse Survey," *Centers for Disease Control and Prevention*, https://www.cdc.-gov/nchs/covid19/pulse/mental-health.htm.

[8] Joe Rubino, "Designing a Future Marked by High Self-Esteem," *Center for Personal Reinvention*, https://www.centerforpersonalreinvention.com/SEA-designing-your-future-with-high-self-esteem.html.

Ch 10 The Hope of His Calling

[1] Jay Lockhart and David L. Roper, *Ephesians and Philippians*, Truth for Today Commentary (Searcy, AR: Resource Publications, 2009), 85.

[2] Darrell L. Bock, *Ephesians: An Introduction and Commentary*, Tyndale New Testament Commentaries 10 (London: Inter-Varsity Press, 2019), 43.

[3] Bauer et al., eds., "ἐλπίς," *BDAG*, 319.

[4] S. S. Smalley, "Joy," *NBD*, 3rd ed., ed. D.R.W. Wood et al. (Downers Grove, IL: InterVersity Press, 1996), 615.

Ch 12 This is the Power of Christ in Me!

[1] Bryan Chapell, *Ephesians* (Phillipsburg, NJ: P&R Publishing, 2009), 123–25.

[2] "Elisabeth Elliot." *The Elisabeth Elliot Foundation.* 2023. https://elisabethelliot.org/.

[3] Elisabeth Elliot, *Keep a Quiet Heart* (Ann Arbor, MI: Servant Publications, 1995), 20.

Appendix A

[1] Leona Atkinson, *54 Spiritual Blessings in Christ: As Found in the Book of Ephesians*, [No location identified]: CreateSpace Independent Publishing, 2011.

Acknowledgments

I almost didn't include these because I'm afraid I'll leave someone out or thank people in the wrong order. I just can't let this book be published, though, without acknowledging the people who propelled it to get to this point. This three-year dream of mine has finally come to fruition. It has moved much more slowly than some preferred (including myself), but I've learned about how this process works.

Thank you to Cypress Publications for believing in this project and the need for women's materials to be available and accessible in the church. Jamie Cox, Bill Bagents, and Brad McKinnon have answered a million questions with the utmost patience. Their guidance and nudging are why this book exists. Thank you to Jamie for getting the book into the format that I envisioned, even with all the changes we made along the way.

To the chapter contributors, it has been a pleasure to work with each of you, and I appreciate your patience and understanding as I was feeling my way through the process. You all were chosen because of the great example you are to me and the church, and I know others will be blessed by your words.

One of the most exciting parts of putting this book together was the opportunity to involve members of my family. My daughter Kait contributed heavily to the prayers and reflection questions you've encountered in each chapter. Her thoughtfulness and eager desire to do God's will are felt through her words. My talented daughter-in-law Ashley designed and produced the cover of the book. She took my wild musings that didn't make much sense even in my own head and created the beautiful product you hold in your hands today. A big thanks to the rest of the family, especially my husband Adam, for being sounding boards and sacrificing time together for the work that went into getting this book published.

To my office assistant Courtney Patterson, thank you for keeping things afloat while I buried my head in this project. And a special shout-out to Homeside Restaurant in Florence, Alabama, for letting me sit at "my booth" for hours on end planning and writing.

And finally, this book would have NEVER made it to press without the diligent work of Melissa McFerrin. She was my rock throughout, being a cheerleader when I needed it and pushing me to step it up when I was being lazy. I leaned more on her expertise than I intended, but she never turned me away. She spent hours proofreading and formatting each chapter, and the finished project is polished because of her.

Autumn Richardson

Contributors

Editors

Melissa McFerrin is the Executive Assistant to the President and Coordinator of Women's Continuing Education at Heritage Christian University. She loves to read, travel, and spend time with her husband, Clay, and their Christian family at the Chisholm Hills Church of Christ.

Autumn Richardson (MMin) is the Director of Distance Learning, an Instructor of Ministry, and Assistant Coordinator of Women's Education at Heritage Christian University. She and her husband Adam worship with the Petersville Church of Christ in Florence, Alabama, and have three adult children, a daughter-in-love, and a granddaughter.

Contributors

Keli M. Brothers, (EdD, LPC-S) is an Assistant Professor of Clinical Mental Health Counseling at the University of North Alabama and an Adjunct Instructor of Psychology at Heritage Christian University. She and her husband, Jeffrey, have two daughters, and serve at Mission of Mercy Church in Florence, Alabama.

Lori Boyd is a registered nurse and teacher. She has authored several Bible study books for women and speaks regularly at ladies' events. She is currently pursuing a Master of Arts in Christian Scripture at Heritage Christian University. Lori and her husband Sam live in Murfreesboro, Tennessee with their three children and are members of the East Main Church of Christ.

Kim Chalmers (MMin) is a former educator and holds a Master of Ministry from HCU with an emphasis in Ministerial Counseling. She lives in Huntsville, Alabama with her husband, Michael, and they worship with the West Huntsville congregation. They have a son, Adam, and daughter-in-law, Cynthia.

Teddy Copeland is a former newspaper reporter and missionary. She loves studying the Scriptures and is in her fifth decade of teaching ladies. Current roles include elder's wife and Gran to six littles!

Debbie Dupuy lives in Florence, Alabama, and is a frequent ladies' day speaker and the author of several study books. Debbie hosts a private Facebook women's group, **Read through the Gospels in 40 Days.** She is passionate about teaching women, sharing Jesus, and assisting her husband with Liberte' Ministries. She and her husband, Arvy, have worked in Haiti for twenty-three years. Debbie is the mother of two daughters and grandmother to three granddaughters.

Jeanne Foust (MA) recently joined the Heritage Christian University faculty as an Instructor of English after a twenty-five-year career in the secondary English classroom. She and her husband work and worship with the Cross Point Church of Christ in Florence, Alabama and have two grown daughters and a son-in-law.

Jodi Gallagher is a mom to six wonderful children, three of whom have been adopted. She lives in Florence, Alabama with her husband, Ed, and children where they attend Sherrod Avenue Church of Christ.

Betty Hamblen (PhD) is a former department director and instructor for Heritage Christian University who, after retirement, spent ten years serving the university as a board member. Betty and her husband, Willie, work and worship with the South Jackson Church of Christ in Houston, Mississippi. They have four children and five grandchildren.

Stacy Harmon (MLIS) is the Library Media Specialist at Mars Hill Bible School in Florence, Alabama, where she has also taught girls' Bible, computer, and Spanish classes. She and her husband, Travis, worship with the Collinwood (TN) Church of Christ, where Travis is the minister. They have two adult daughters, a son-in-law, a beautiful granddaughter named Evelynn, and a Morkie named Thor.

Kait Richardson is pursuing a degree in Social Work from the University of North Alabama. She lives in Florence, Alabama, and works with victims of domestic violence.

Rosemary Snodgrass (PhD) is a licensed professional counselor. She transitioned from a successful career as a school counselor to teaching both graduate and undergraduate courses for Heritage Christian University. Before retiring, she served as director of the Alpha Center, a Christian counseling center, in Florence, Alabama. Her husband, Don, is an elder with the Sherrod Avenue Church of Christ. Rosemary has taught counseling courses in the Philippians and South Africa.

Lori Tays (MBA) is Vice President for External Relations at Mars Hill Bible School in Florence, Alabama. She holds an Executive MBA from the University of North Alabama and a B.A. in Biblical Studies from Heritage Christian University. Lori and her son, Brennan, worship with the Killen Church of Christ.

Cathy Turner is a 20-year columnist for the Courier-Journal with a bimonthly column about family, entitled

"Cat and Kids." She teaches ladies and girls all over the southeast including at Wood Avenue Church of Christ in Florence, Alabama, where her husband is an elder. They have three children, four grandchildren.

Credits

Select Scripture quotations are taken from the NEW KING JAMES VERSION®. Copyright© 1982 by Thomas Nelson, Inc. Used by permission. All rights reserved.

Select Scriptures quotations are taken from the Holy Bible, New International Version®, NIV®. Copyright © 1973, 1978, 1984, 2011 by Biblica, Inc.™ Used by permission of Zondervan. All rights reserved worldwide. www.zondervan.com The "NIV" and "New International Version" are trademarks registered in the United States Patent and Trademark Office by Biblica, Inc.®

Scripture quotations are from the ESV® Bible (The Holy Bible, English Standard Version®), copyright © 2001 by Crossway, a publishing ministry of Good News Publishers. Used by permission. All rights reserved.

Scripture quotations taken from the (NASB®) New American Standard Bible®, Copyright © 1960, 1971,

God's warmth in our hearts. His light in our lives.

Our Mission

Radiant exists for the purpose of cultivating spiritual formation within the hearts of women. We equip women by providing theologically rich resources and opportunities to serve and study scripture.

Our Vision

Radiant women look to Him in all areas of life and are transformed into the image of Christ.

Scan to learn more about Radiant or visit www.hcu.edu/resources/church-resources/womens-resources/!

Also by Cypress Publications

Hamblen, Betty. *Women in the Shadows* (2022)

Berean Study Series

Led by God's Spirit: A Practical Study of Galatians 5:22–26 (2023)

Majesty and Mercy: God Through the Eyes of Isaiah (2022)

For the Glory of God: Christ and the Church in Ephesians (2021)

Cloud of Witnesses: Ancient Stories of Faith (2020)

Visions of Grace (2019)

Instructions for Living: The Ten Commandments (2018)

Clothed in Christ: A How-to Guide (2017)

What Does Real Christianity Look Like? A Study of the Parables (2016)

The Ekklesia of Christ: Becoming the People of God (2015)

To see full catalog of Heritage Christian University Press
and its imprint Cypress Publications, visit
www.hcu.edu/publications